Holy Mirth: A Theology of Laughter

Richard G. Cote

D1599029

Affirmation Books
House of Affirmation
Whitinsville, Massachusetts

Published with ecclesiastical permission

First Edition
© 1986 by House of Affirmation, Inc.

Library of Congress Cataloging in Publication Data

Cote, Richard G., 1934-
   Holy Mirth

   1. Laughter—Religious aspects—Christianity. I. Title.
BT709.C67   1986   233   86-14166
ISBN 0-89571-031-5

Cover design by Marian Bates

Printed by
The Alpine Press, Stoughton, Massachusetts
United States of America

Table of Contents

Dedication

For my sisters and brothers

Ted
Edna
Rita
Rachel
Edmund
Paul

for whom a good laugh
was always
a sign of love

Foreword

Affirmation Books usually publishes books that combine psychology and theology. Humor is the meeting place of the human and divine; it affirms our humanity and the possibilities God gives us in life for growth. Humor deals with the emotions so it is a psychological subject. Since theology can (or should be) applied to all aspects of life it is fitting to talk about a theology of humor.

We badly need humor in today's world. It reminds us of our fragility, weakness, and humanness. It opens the door to humility by inviting us not to take ourselves so seriously. Humor is a gift to the Church, and the author, Fr. Richard Cote, helps us to reflect on this gift. After reading this book the words of Christ take on significant meaning for the contemporary Christian. "I have told you this so that my own joy may be in you and your joy may be complete" (John 15:11).

It is my hope that this newest publication of Affirmation Books may challenge the thought and encourage the faith of its readers.

Thomas A. Kane, Ph.D., D.P.S.
Priest, Diocese of Worcester
Publisher, Affirmation Books
Natick, Massachusetts

6 August 1986
Feast of the Transfiguration

Introduction

At the outset of a theological reflection such as this, it is accepted practice to say that one has something important to offer, that one is confident the reader will want to hear it, and that the end result will be rewarding. I am therefore at a threefold disadvantage: (a) a theology of laughter will not be immediately perceived as something that touches upon the essence of our Christian faith; (b) some readers will be reluctant to replace their traditional image of a solemn God with a laughing and humorous God, and (c) those who are able to make this shift in their sacred symbols of God may get more than they bargained for — they may have to change their lives, and this, as we all know, can be a disquieting experience.

From the days of the early Church until now, Christians have often been suspicious of laughter. "Be sober and vigilant" has been our motto. I remember my mother telling me when I was growing up, "Don't laugh so much because you'll end up crying before the day is over." People often think that in laughter they risk being irresponsible. The perversions of laughter have been judged more severely than the pitfalls of solemnity. It is safer to spend one's time in "serious" activity than to enter into "frivolity."

However, Christians are rediscovering the need to laugh, perhaps because we find so little to laugh about in the world today. Or it may be we are learning God has a sense of humor after all. Whatever the reason, laughter certainly offers freedom to the human spirit and never before have Christians seemed more bent on being free. In a world in which our biggest fears gravitate toward the extremes of real ulcers or feigned apathy, laughter becomes the possibility of discovering our common humanity. In a world in which so much can and often does go wrong, Christian laughter can become a new way of possessing our faith. In a time when even our popes and theologians take themselves very seriously, Christian theology is being challenged to reassess its suspicion of laughter.

One of the amazing things about laughter is that unlike other human reflexes, it harbors a wisdom all its own. We commonly assume that any person who can laugh wholeheartedly cannot be irreclaimably bad. Where there is laughter, there is always hope: some wild dream that it is possible for God to love us as we really are — warts and all. And is it not also true that we feel something is wrong when laughter is excluded from any area of human life? The human condition is serious, but it is also funny, sometimes very funny, and we feel a person who cannot laugh is either sick, disturbed, or "not all there."

This attempt to articulate a theology of laughter will strike some people as whimsical, yet it can hardly come as a surprise. In recent years we have witnessed a proliferation of "theologies" — for instance, a secular theology, a "death-of-God" theology, a theology of hope, a theology of liberation, a theology of story. But a theology of laughter? Is this not pushing things a bit too far? The reader may even be tempted to put this book down and read no farther, were it not for the fact that this, too, is one of the paradoxes and saving graces of human laughter: it redeems what might otherwise be lost.

It should also be clear from the start that our theology of laughter makes no apology for raising eyebrows and disconcerting people. In fact, it deliberately seeks to create mental jolts and catch people off guard, thus challenging — even threatening — some of our basic spiritual values, beliefs, and attitudes. In this sense, a theology of laughter is a "subversive" theology: it not only dares to laugh at everything we take for granted, everything that appears to make sense, but it also subverts our understanding of human progress. More important, it allows God to creep back into our secular world, and this divine intrusion is not without its own subversive and humorous results.

Let me begin with a brief statement on how I envisage the theological task, particularly as it relates to the phenomenon of laughter. My point of departure for a theology of laughter can be expressed as follows: things have a depth dimension that only faith can see — their being is from God and toward God. God is both the origin and the goal of everything that is, including human laughter. Hence even our laughter touches the Divine with the fringes of its being. The person who meets laughter reverently, who accepts it as a sacred reality and not just as a human reflex, honors its mystery which is grounded in God.

My contention is not that laughter is an infallible sign of God's presence, but rather that God's presence invariably makes us want to laugh. There is something about God, something about Divine folly that strikes us funny. In the final analysis, we laugh because God laughs. Laughter, we know, is not stable and permanent: it is fleeting and ungraspable, and it comes to us only when we do not expect it, when we are surprised into it. In those special moments of vulnerability, we often gain a deeper insight into what God wants to be for us today and the glory that is already ours in hope.

The basic thesis of this study is that humor is an integral dimension of Christian faith, and to have lost a sense of humor — whether in Christian living, spirituality, or theology — is to have lost a vital element of our faith. I will examine the connection between faith and the comic spirit, and suggest that we must learn to laugh at the human predicament in which every genuine act of faith places us. Only when God's divine sense of humor is acknowledged and becomes truly integrated in our spirituality can the Church hope to preach the Good News to a troubled world with any real hope of contagious results.

My study begins with a look at why Christians find it difficult to laugh in today's world (chapter 1), and why Jesus has never been seriously portrayed as one who could and probably did laugh heartily (chapter 2). I then review some recent theological developments that have helped to pave the way for a theology of laughter (chapter 3). I also examine how God's own sense of humor comes through to us in Scripture as well as in our response to God's word (chapters 4 and 5). Having thus secured the foundations of the theology, I then suggest, in chapter 6, a more fully developed theology of laughter. The remaining three chapters work out some practical applications of this theology and what it might mean for our life of faith and Christian ministry.

Every effort has been made to write this book in non-sexist language. I wish to disclaim any sexist intent where — and only for the sake of simplicity of style — God is referred to as 'him'.

In addition, I should like to express my thanks to Sister Marie Kraus, executive editor of Affirmation Books, for her suggestions and encouragement. I would also like to thank Ann Wald, assistant editor, for her ideas and support in preparing the manuscript. Her own enthusiasm became contagious just when it was most needed.

Richard G. Cote, O.M.I.

Is it possible to laugh in today's world? 1

It is very hard to sustain humor, or the desire for humor, in a period when we seem to be trying, on the one hand, to invent a pill or a miracle drug that will cure us of everything, and on the other hand to invent machines for instant annihilation.

— James Thurber

LAUGHTER DOES NOT COME EASILY in today's world. The negative trends in American society — trends that could lead us to believe that the American dream is an illusory hope — make laughter difficult. Every day we see more confusion and debate over morality and traditional values. Newspaper headlines and television screens bring disturbing news about corruption in government, business, sports, and educational institutions into our homes.

Recent surveys indicate, for example, that crime in the U.S. is endemic. One out of every five American citizens has been mugged, robbed, assaulted, or had his or her home burglarized at least once during the past year. It is estimated that alcohol abuse accounts for thousands of domestic disputes, homicides, and traffic fatalities. One person in five claims to know of at least one case of child or spouse abuse in the immediate neighborhood.

We are aware that nearly half of America's marriages end in divorce, and that each year more than a million American teenagers become pregnant, four out of five of them unmarried. Unemployment among young people is also extremely high, and the poor are still very much with us. In fact, some thirty-two million Americans are defined as poor, earning less than $9,287 for a family of four. The public, moreover, has been disillusioned by the inability of the government and other social institutions to solve these problems. We have the lowest voting record of any major democracy in the world, and our continuing negative image of politics and politicians reflects our lack of confidence in the political system.

There is little in this information that would prompt anyone to laugh — and we have not even mentioned the tragedies, global conflicts, and disasters that have become our steady diet in the press and on television's nightly news. All of these events affect our frame of mind and emotional climate, making it difficult for us to sustain humor and a comic vision.

Nor do we find much relief in the kind of humor we commonly encounter, American humor. We know that laughter in its highest expression is a healing power. Dr. Raymond Moody's best seller *Laugh After Laugh* and *The Laughter Prescription* by Dr. Lawrence Peter have recently reminded us of this, as have the tireless efforts of educator-psychologist Leo Buscaglia. But we also know that laughter can be a destructive force, one that goes for the jugular, as it were, instead of to the heart. For some reason, American humor is particularly prone to this tendency and is often used as a means of self-justification.

Louis Kronenberger observed this defensive trait in our American humor. "We don't make fun of ourselves," he said, "only of our minorities and failures, of those who don't conform or assert themselves or measure up. Our humor, where it is directed inward and not at mere 'goats,' is almost completely flattering."[1] Whenever we do joke about our shortcomings, weaknesses, and failures there is a stilted air of contrived greatness behind our humor. Our put-downs are often an ill-disguised form of self-congratulation. Typical examples are when Cher pokes fun at her flat chest, when

Phyllis Diller says, "I've just spent four afternoons at the beauty parlor — for an estimate," or when Joan Rivers, who plays the part of an anguish-ridden female verging on spinsterhood despite her mother's zealous efforts relates, "When an unmarried orthopedic surgeon moved in next door, my mother slammed the piano lid on my fingers." The comic portrayals of Lucille Ball, Carol Burnett, Archie Bunker, Richard Pryor, and Eddie Murphy all have a heavily defensive quality.

In our own speech what may be superficially interpreted as intentional self-criticism appears, upon closer analysis, as boastful self-justification. Our confessions of weakness and failure are often breezy attempts to write them off. Our self-deprecating humor, as Kronenberger puts it, "is almost a way of serving notice on people that we may misbehave. We announce that we are part of the rat race as we might announce that we are part of the general public; we dub ourselves bastards as fair warning that we may be expected to behave as such."[2]

In addition, most American comedians portray victims of one kind or another. The victims are usually of two kinds: aggressive or passive. Don Rickles, for example, playing "Paranoid Urban Man" is a frustrated and aggressive victim who flails through life until he finally collapses from sheer exhaustion. Woody Allen is the passive victim when he brings a real moose to a costume party and the animal gets second prize, the winner being the Berkowitzes dressed in a tasteless moose costume. You just can't win! Rodney Dangerfield plays the family-man victim: "I asked my wife to run away with me. She said, 'You go.'" Or again when he complains, "My son goes to a private school. I've been trying for three years to get him to tell me where it is." All our victims seem to be saying, "We can't handle life by ourselves." Their anxious humor reflects the negative trends referred to earlier, a loss of confidence in the forces of goodness, order, and love. Lenny Bruce once said that all his humor was based on destruction and despair. One of the few exceptions is the humor of Bill Cosby, which may explain its popular appeal and high television ratings.

So the question remains: can the comic vision and Christian faith really be reconciled? Can a sense of humor form the basis of a genuine Christian spirituality? The answer, I think, is yes.

Christian laughter is not incompatible with the potential pain of human contradictions, the inherent discrepancies and muddiness of the human condition, or the ambiguities of truth and goodness. On the contrary, one of the uncanny things our faith teaches us is to welcome the world we know and suffer in with sobriety and delight, with a sort of serene and playful acquiescence. In doing so we find God has welcomed this world before any of us, in spite of us. The laughter of faith makes sense only if the darker side of life is also met with full recognition. Even when the situation at hand is tragic, the Christian remains in touch with the promise of Christ's final victory and knows that nothing of everlasting value will be utterly destroyed and absolutely lost. Although we may feel the burdens and darkness of the world acutely, the laughter of faith enables us to love the world God loves and yet not confide ultimately in it. Christian life has never flourished in a mood of unrelenting seriousness. Rather, it thrives in an atmosphere of serious joyfulness — the kind called for by our Lord when he invites us to be fully in the world, but not of the world.[3] Such is the comic burden of our faith. When Christians fail to take up this burden, and live by other visions instead, then the "salt of the earth" loses much of its tang.

Church in a new mode

There can be no doubt that it is difficult to laugh in today's world. For a Christian, however, the difficulty lies not only in the kind of world in which we live, but also in the kind of church in which we believe.

In pre-Vatican II days, Catholics had a buoyant confidence in themselves and their Church. They were proud to belong to a worldwide Church with a tightly ordered hierarchy, a Church with a rich tradition, a clear, unified doctrinal system, and an impressive record of shaping the history of Christian Europe. They loved their Church and were prepared to defend it. This ecclesial self-confidence, developed over the centuries, was nourished by almost everything connected with the Church—its rules, procedures, worship, address, and theology. By any reckoning, it was a superior Church. And even if the Church made generous use of pomp, power, and prestige, its intention was "for the greater glory of God and the salvation of souls."

Now the picture is different. Within a few short years, or so it now seems, the image of the Church has changed dramatically. The Church now defines itself as a servant community and is mindful of its growing minority status in a large and complex world. Many religious practices, once thought permanent, have been called into question. Many teachings, once thought definitive, have undergone intense scrutiny and criticism. Many hesitations, once carefully hidden, have now surfaced into the broad daylight of public debate. Catholics have come to realize that the Church does not have ready answers for the queries and torments that beset the world today. They no longer experience their faith as a "package deal," a body of truths they can possess and with which they are satisfied. In an age of religious triumphalism, it might have been feasible to develop a theology of laughter; but in the present ecclesial context is it possible? With the church's diminished sense of importance, are there not fewer occasions to laugh? Would not such a spirituality go against the way Christians are expected to live their faith in a deeply troubled world?

The historical context does of course affect the Church's ability—or inability—to laugh. Yet the ability to laugh at the dilemmas in which we find ourselves still remains one of the greatest assets a Christian can possess. The laughter of faith transcends any image or model we may have of the Church and we need to discern something of God's incredible sense of humor in our times. I am not suggesting we return to triumphalism. It has become a pejorative word in Christian circles and it is not likely to be rehabilitated in our lifetime. Nor do I advise that we go back to the fleshpots of religious imperialism. Our challenge today is more straightforward: as Christians we must learn to laugh in our new servant role.

From a Christian point of view, service and superiority, though incongruous, are not incompatible. In fact, they go together and form an important creative tension within the life of faith itself. Laughter thrives on incongruity, and in the basic tension between Christian service and superiority the urge to laugh is heightened, not diminished. We must not discard one of the horns of the dilemma (either humble service or the feeling of superiority), but rather integrate them both into our life of faith. Jesus himself gives us a good example of how this is done in the way he experienced the roles of master and servant.

Jesus is Lord—he knows it and says so (Luke 22:27); he is master—he knows it and says so (Matt. 10:25). Even when he removes the distance of superiority that separates him from his disciples, he still underlines it, "A servant is not greater than his master. If they persecuted me, they will persecute you too" (John 15:20). Yet his lordship lies in his taking upon himself the humiliating and finally killing task of a servant. He came "not to be served but to serve" (Matt. 20:28). In the gospel, Jesus is absolute master and absolute servant, or in Karl Barth's words, "the Lord as servant and the servant as Lord." He can allow himself to be a servant while remaining the master, and he does not cease to be the Lord when he is a servant. We find something of the same creative tension and incongruity in the formula for action which Jesus gives his disciples, "Be cunning as serpents, and harmless as doves" (Matt. 10:16). Seldom do we find the humble assertive, or the assertive humble. But this balance of opposites is precisely the paradox for which Jesus calls.

Nothing less is required for developing a Christian sense of humor. Only when service and superiority are held in creative tension can a Christian hope to embrace service as a way of life and laughter as a spirituality. A Christian who does not feel privileged or superior in being called to a commitment of service will not do much liberating—or laughing. The reason is simple: the high demands of service — good service — are such that if we have a poor self-image or a sense of inferiority, we cannot be "generative" (in Erikson's sense of the term), ready to use our time, our talents, our energies, and all that we are and have for the benefit of others. So there is a sense in which superiority and service are not mutually exclusive. Indeed whenever we integrate them properly into our spiritual life, our Christian service gains an unexpected power of its own, as with Mother Teresa of Calcutta, to touch the hearts of people at a depth far beyond ordinary human assistance. And our laughter, like that of good Pope John, is again heard both in and outside the Church.

Theories of laughter

Another fact that must not be overlooked is that no one has yet devised an adequate theory of laughter. Many attempts have been made to explain why people laugh. Yet despite the fact that human laughter has been observed, studied, and researched from every angle, it remains something of a mystery and subject to numerous interpretations.[4] Human laughter has been defined as an overflow of "surplus nervous energy" (Spencer), a sort of "cheerful sneeze" (Boudes), an "antidote to sympathy" (McDougall), or a "momentary anaesthesia of the heart" (Bergson). Alexander Bain, a nineteenth-century pioneer of experimental psychology, claimed that the urge to laugh is present "whenever a person can achieve a stroke of superiority, in surpassing or discomforting a rival." This would explain, so his theory goes, why we laugh at other's mistakes, handicaps, misfortunes, or idiosyncrasies. Sigmund Freud, on the other hand, believed that humor allows us to vent our aggressive or sexual feelings and anxieties in a disguised manner, while George Milner explains it as a built-in safety device which keeps us from becoming either too beastly or too sophisticated. Others have suggested that we laugh in order to release tension, to weaken criticism, or to insure a minimum of spiritual communion and conviviality with our neighbor.

Without denying that there may be some truth (and even a touch of humor) in all these solemn theories, laughter remains a mystery. As Arthur Koestler put it: "To find the explanation why we laugh may be a task as delicate as analyzing the chemical composition of a perfume, with its multiple ingredients — some of which are never perceived, while others, sniffed in isolation, would make us wince."[5]

We need a different approach that begins by accepting laughter as a *sacred* mystery. All the above theories explain the phenomenon of laughter by looking "down" instead of "up" — down, that is, into the depths of the human psyche. They do not conceive that human laughter might be a reflection from on high, a reflection of something God does with infinitely more gusto and spontaneity than we do — in short, that laughter is truly divine.

What we laugh at and why, and what moves us to formalize our mirth in jokes and comedy, can perhaps best be understood as a sympathetic vibration of God's heavenly laughter — a laughter that tells us that, in spite of everything, all is well. Our laughter is but a quiver, a childlike reverberation of God's own laughter. Ultimately, we laugh because God laughs. Laughter is a divine attribute and finds only a faint echo in our hearts and on our lips. When we laugh we do not really know what we are doing. But we feel Someone is keeping an eye on our vital interests, so it is safe to close both our eyes in laughter, or wink at one another over our earthly fortunes and misfortunes. Sociologist Peter Berger quite rightly sees in humor "a rumor of angels" and a "hint of the transcendent" — in short, a divine signal of what it means to be human.[6] Laughter is a blunt, brilliant, brave affirmation on the part of humankind that death is not the final answer. We seek a vision of the place where this joy and this laughter are everlasting. Only when viewed from this perspective, as a sacred mystery, does human laughter disclose its true meaning and beauty.

The Bible tells us that we were created in the image of God. Christian tradition has always taken this notion of "image of God" as the only real basis for understanding the human being. It is an angle of vision in which each of us, male or female, can most fittingly be said to be "like" God. The sense of this mystery becomes both the condition and the criterion for getting hold of truth—and this includes the truth about laughter. As the present study will attempt to show, we not only share in the goodness and perfection of God; we also share in God's mirth and comic spirit. We are gifted, as no other creature on earth, with the ability to laugh, the power to "see through" human situations, and, for a few brief moments at least, to experience something of God's own incredible sense of humor.

Endnotes

1. Louis Kronenberg, *Company Manners: A Cultural Inquiry into Modern American Life* (New York: Bobbs-Merrill, 1962), p. 166.
2. Ibid., p. 169.
3. See John 17:14-15.
4. For the many theories on the nature and origin of the sense of humor, see J.C. Flugel, "Humor and Laughter," *Handbook of Social Psychology*, ed. Gardner Lindzey, vol. 2 (Reading, Mass.: Addison-Wesley, 1954), pp. 709-734. See also Edmund Bergier, *Laughter and the Sense of Humor* (New York: International Medical Book Corporation, 1956), pp. 2-41.
5. Arthur Koestler, *The Act of Creation* (New York: Macmillan, 1964), p. 61.
6. Peter Berger, *A Rumor of Angels* (Garden City, N.Y.: Doubleday, 1970), pp. 69-72.

"Jesus never laughed" 2

> *I wonder why you are so opposed to the
> idea that Jesus may have laughed.*
> —William in Umberto Eco's novel
> *The Name of the Rose*

RELIGION IS SELDOM a laughing matter. It is taken seriously by both those who believe and those who do not. In fact, religion is one area of human life where laughter is generally frowned upon. Laughter, at least hearty laughter, is viewed as being the opposite of holiness. This idea is reinforced by certain biblical texts. "A fool raises his voice in laughter," we are told in the Book of Sirach, "but the wise person, at most, smiles discreetly" (21:20).

For Old Testament writers and rabbis, laughter had a pagan ring because the Canaanite gods and goddesses laughed and made merry. In sharp contrast to these pagan deities, Yahweh was portrayed as more forbidding, devoid of any trace of gaiety and geniality. The only concession the biblical writers made was the acceptance of the laughter of derision: "He who sits in the heavens laughs, the Lord derides them" (Ps. 2:4). Only scornful laughter was compatible with Yahweh's severity toward those who refuse to obey.

In addition, the tendency of ancient humor was to laugh at rather than to laugh with people. Much of the laughter described in the Bible is the laughter of scorn and contempt. The humor of the ancient Israelites victimized somebody, whether it was the idols of the neighboring peoples whose powerlessness before Yahweh they found ridiculous (I Sam. 5:2-5), or the neighboring peoples themselves, with their strange names and odd appearance (Gen. 25:25), or enemies defeated by popular Israelite heroes. In each of the four instances in the Old Testament where God laughs,[1] the laughter is depicted as a contemptuous reaction to the ways of the wicked on earth. God is provoked to laughter because humans take themselves and their plottings so seriously. Divine laughter is meant to convey God's superiority, not sense of humor.

In the New Testament, humor is also rarely described. Even where the joy and gladness that characterize the life of a Christian are mentioned, the Greek word used *(chairo)* refers to a restrained and chastened joy rather than one that breaks out in peals of laughter.

The real problem, of course, is that the gospels do not tell us that Jesus laughed. They speak of the Lord's tears, but do not record his smiles. Jesus got angry, he grew tired, he was sorely tempted, but there is not a word about his laughing or even smiling. It would be difficult to exaggerate the importance of this omission in the eyes of first century Christians. For many Church Fathers, like Clement of Alexandria, Ephrem, Basil, John Chrysostom, Jerome, and Augustine, this silence was a compelling reason why Christians should not laugh. Tears, not laughter, should mark our pilgrim journey here on earth, they thought. They also based their teaching on a literal interpretation of our Lord's warning: "Woe to you who laugh, for you shall weep" (Luke 6:25). Typical of such early forebodings is the one found in John Chrysostom's homily: "Laughter does not seem to be a sin, but it leads to sin." From the start, then, Christianity discouraged spurious laughter and mirth, a tradition that continued through the Middle Ages and into the seventeenth and eighteenth centuries. In a treatise on this subject in 1694, the French bishop and writer, Jacques Bossuet condemned laughter, as so many had before him, on moral grounds as well as on the authority of Paul and the early Church writers. This solemn opinion was even enshrined in a popular maxim: "Only with trepidation does the wise person laugh" *(Le sage ne rit qu'en trem-blant)*. Two centuries later, in 1855, author Charles Baudelaire defended what he called "the essentially Christian nature" of this maxim.[2] In doing so, he was merely echoing a long-standing tradition among Christians.

Despite the lack of any explicit evidence that Jesus laughed, one wonders why the idea was never seriously entertained. Why this reluctance to think that Jesus, on occasion, laughed heartily? After all, even where the gospels are silent about the personal life of Jesus, as in his early, hidden years, Christians have never been at a loss to fill these information gaps with pious legends and devotional myths. Yet for some reason even popular piety, rarely short on imagination, never cultivated the image of a "laughing Jesus." A smiling infant Jesus, yes; but never an adult Jesus with a spontaneous burst of laughter on his lips. It would be natural for Christians to assume that since Jesus got angry, he could also laugh. Such an assumption seems all the more reasonable if one recalls that theologians of the past were inclined to speculate and often debated such hypothetical questions. Not so. The only known exception was medieval theologian Peter Cantor, who suggested that Jesus probably laughed since he was a real human being. This line of reasoning, however, never became popular because it was contrary to the contemporary religious sensitivities.

There are several reasons why Christians were reluctant to attribute laughter to Jesus. First, human laughter was held in low esteem. The ancient Greeks excluded laughter from their ideal of moral perfection, mainly because they perceived comedy as essentially cruel. Plato said we laugh at the misfortunes of our friends. Aristotle considered laughter as a kind of derangement and deception. Cicero believed that we only laugh at something base and dishonorable. In the biographies of Anaxagoras, Heraclitus,

Socrates, Plato, and Cato the Younger, we are expressly told that these great philosophers never laughed once—a biographical detail probably intended to prove further their moral rectitude and greatness. Thus early Christian writers were quick to point out that Jesus never laughed. His abstention from laughter was one way to demonstrate his superior wisdom and stature.

Another, more serious, reason why laughter could not be attributed to Jesus was its close association with the Devil, the prince of lies. Laughter can of course be strained, cruel, artificial, and deceptive. It can mask our true feelings or our real intentions. In an era when the malicious nature of human laughter is preeminent, it is not surprising that laughter came to be seen as a characteristic of Satan. From early Christian to late medieval models, devils were imagined as rough humanoid bipeds bestially deformed, horned, with goat's shanks, cloven hooves, spiked tails, and grotesque smirks on their faces. In contrast, Jesus was portrayed as the "man of sorrows." The contrast was deliberate and profoundly theological; it underscored the enormous rivalry that existed between these two antagonists who were locked in bitter struggle for dominion over the human race. Within this cosmic duel, laughter came to have a force and a power all its own—that of a functional myth. Symbolically, it embodied all the devilish traits of cunning, trickery, and ruse, and thereby acquired a fear-inducing quality all its own. In such a mythical context, laughter could scarcely be legitimized by Christians, much less attributed to Jesus. Laughter was demonic and dangerous; it had to be controlled, restrained, disciplined, held in check.

A third reason why Christians could scarcely believe that Jesus laughed hinges on their conception of Jesus' knowledge. The notion was long common among theologians that from the first moment of his conception Jesus possessed complete knowledge of the world and the people he was to redeem. Not only that, he could read into our hearts and see right through our tangled webs of human motives. Quite apart from the fact that such a view makes a sham of Jesus' genuine humanity, it all but precludes the possibility of humor. This is true at least in the common understanding of what makes things funny. Is a joke humorous if we already know the punch line? Is it possible to make others laugh if we cannot surprise them or if they know it all?

Today we think differently and more kindly about human laughter. Even so, Christians still have difficulty accepting the idea that laughter might be divine or sacred. There is a persistent feeling that laughter has more to do with the world of flesh than the kingdom of God, more with our worldly-mindedness than with our life of faith. The "demons" of human laughter are not yet completely exorcized. Religion continues to be regarded as a deeply serious matter that has little to do with genuine laughter.

Our life of faith is serious, and we must not forget that. But it is also funny, inherently funny; we must not forget that either. We live in a generation that seems to have forgotten—and perhaps never knew—the incredible humor and foolishness of God. It is difficult for us to espouse a genuine spirituality of laughter.

Today, our Christian misgivings come at several levels. First, there is the ethical misgiving. Christians might instinctively feel that laughter is an inappropriate response to the world's problems. Only serious dedication and sacrifice, and perhaps angry protest, will rid the world of war, racism, hunger, and injustice. How can we laugh when so much is still harsh, terrible, and evil around us, when so many people still have to worry about the necessities of life? How can Christians be expected, much less encouraged, to laugh when the dignity of the human person is so often misunderstood or misinterpreted, when the entire human community lives under the threat of nuclear annihilation?

A second level of misgiving is ecclesial. As I said earlier, our misgivings about a spirituality of laughter stem in part from the kind of church in which we believe. In the years following Vatican II, the Catholic Church experienced some profound and deeply disturbing changes: massive resignations from the priesthood, a sharp decline in vocations and religious practice, and erosion of the credibility of ecclesiastical authority. Many people had to grapple with the role of the institutional church in their Christian identity. They questioned whether they could identify with certain practices and policies of the Church which they perceived to be unjust. Is it any wonder, then, that most Catholics would hesitate to associate the comic spirit with their faith or their Church? To see the glory of God in a weak, human Church struggling to renew itself in the Spirit is not easy. For someone who really loves the Church, can it ever be funny?

Finally, there is a theological misgiving, illustrated by a quote from Reinhold Niebuhr. In the concluding passage of his essay, "Humor and Faith," he states: "Insofar as the sense of humor is a recognition of incongruity, it is more profound than any philosophy which seeks to devour incongruity in reason. But the sense of humor remains healthy only when it deals with immediate issues and faces the obvious and surface irrationalities. It must move toward faith or sink into despair when ultimate issues are raised. That is why there is laughter in the vestibule of the temple, the echo of laughter in the temple itself, but only faith and prayer, and no laughter, in the holy of holies."[3] Niebuhr clearly recognizes the value of humor, but he fails to see it as a dimension-in-depth of faith itself. At most, he is prepared to concede that humor can be a prelude to faith, and laughter the beginning of prayer. But this is as far as he is willing to go. For him, faith transcends laughter in the sense that faith goes beyond laughter and somehow leaves it behind. It is fine to laugh at the foibles and trivialities of our everyday lives, but not when we deal with the mighty questions of human existence and our relationship with God.

Such a view raises another vexing problem—can humor ever become more than just a peripheral grace in the pastoral action of the Church? Can it ever become a true working principle in the task of evangelization, informing our missionary vision and Christian outlook? The question is very real if one considers that most attempts to integrate the comic spirit and pastoral action in the past have not been successful. Yet one cannot help wondering (to paraphrase G.K. Chesterton) whether the real problem might not be that such a challenge was found too difficult, and therefore was left untried.

We know, for example, that humor was used purposefully and pastorally by American church leaders in the eighteenth and nineteenth centuries, especially by Protestant ministers. A 1975 study by Doug Adams entitled *Humor in the American Pulpit* assesses the theological significance of humor in American preaching from George Whitefield through Henry Ward Beecher. Adams examines the motives of those who used humor in the pulpit and shows how it was employed in several ways: (1) to attract attention, (2) to cope with intentional or unintentional disruptions, (3) to introduce controversial subjects, (4) to ridicule the arguments of the infidels, and (5) to exorcise the idolatries of power, wisdom, and wealth. Here, at least, we have a pioneering attempt "to put laughter to work in worship." However this pastoral humor remained more of a religious ploy than a genuine spirituality. It was not a dimension-in-depth of either the preacher's faith or message.

In recent years, a growing number of church leaders and scholars have discovered the importance of humor and laughter for the Church and its ministry. Speaking to an international group of catechists and lay teachers in Rome in 1976, the late John Cardinal Wright deplored the lack of laughter and joy in the Church. He noted that this deficiency was undoubtedly one of the main reasons why the Church was having such difficulty in reaching out to youth as well as to adult intellectuals. Echoing this idea, another well-known cleric of our day, Andrew Greeley, has written: "The sort of contagious joy that flows from the laughter of faith is the best guarantee of effective ecclesiastical ministry that can possibly exist. The matter can be put more strongly: The ecclesiastical minister who is not capable of the laughter of faith stands little if any chance of effective use of his or her ministry."[4] Walter Kasper, in his book, *An Introduction to Christian Faith*, is no less emphatic. "One of the main elements of Christian faith is humor, and the lack of humor and the irritability into which we in the contemporary Church and contemporary theology have so often slipped is perhaps one of the most serious objections which can be brought against present-day Christianity."[5]

The Church has always had a few prophets of laughter, a few voices laughing in the wilderness. The greatest in living memory is Pope John XXIII. Not that he ever wrote anything on the spirituality of laughter; he lived it. Integrating humor and pastoral action he showed how laughter can be existentially grounded in faith itself. Pope John's faith ushered in a new era and made laughter possible in the Church. His faith declared — openly and without embarrassment — that it was all right for a pope to be a human being, a weak, sinful, somewhat improbable, overweight, wobbly human being. What others considered unbecoming, inappropriate or subversive, John saw as a possibility of grace, a chance to love and to laugh. He firmly believed that God loves people as they are. For him, laughter was both a necessity and a virtue. As he put it, laughter accompanied him throughout life like a good friend, so that "bliss may be never-ending."

We need to correct our perception of Christian life so we can discover God's own incredible sense of humor. If human existence at times appears absurd, the promptings of the Holy Spirit are often even more disconcerting and laughable. So we must first learn to experience God's humor in our own lives. Only then can we make it available as a source of recognition for others; only then can we hope to proclaim the Good News to the poor with any real conviction and contagiously joyous results. Pastoral action must be carried out under the influence of God's humor because it is here, surprisingly enough, that things reveal their deeper meaning and ultimate beauty.

It would be a sad mistake, however, to think that the spirituality of laughter I suggest can be had cheaply. It is not to be confused with the thin, painted smile we sometimes see on the face of some "comic saints." Nor can it be an easy excuse to shirk the strain of an intense religious life. To harbor such a thought is to misunderstand the demands of the Sermon on the Mount. The kind of humor I speak about here knows all the demands of Christian faith because it is born of that very faith. In the words of Walter Kasper, it is a basic attitude which allows us "to be totally human and only human because it alone allows God to be God and exposes all other claims to absolute status and honor as ridiculous."[6] Christian laughter is concerned first and foremost with God's kingdom in the world, and that, in all truth, cannot be had cheaply.

Endnotes

1. Biblical references to God's laughter: Ps. 2:4, 37:13 and 59:8. See also Prov. 1:26.
2. Charles Baudelaire, *Oeuvres completes: Curiosités esthétiques* (Paris: Louis Conard, 1923), pp. 371-372.
3. Reinhold Niebuhr, *Discerning the Signs of the Times* (New York: Charles Scribner's Sons, 1946) pp. 130-134.
4. Andrew Greeley, "Humor and Ecclesiastical Ministry," *Concilium*, New Series 5 (1974), p. 140.
5. Walter Kasper, *An Introduction to Christian Faith* (Ramsey, N.J.: Paulist Press, 1980), p. 131.
6. Ibid., p. 132.

The quest for holy mirth   3

Theology is a joyful science.
— Karl Barth

IF WE WERE LOOKING for the "family background" or ancestry of a theology of laughter, we would not find any direct line of descent, except perhaps in the lives of the saints. However, a number of significant theological occurrences point in this direction and, when taken together, supply an interesting background to the theology of laughter. Among these are: (1) negative theology, (2) the theology of play, and (3) process theology. My purpose is not to elaborate on these theologies but simply to point out how each brings an important corrective to our traditional understanding of God, and so opens the possibility of imagining a God who can and does laugh. Prior to these theological developments, a theology of laughter could not have been constructed; now its emergence appears inevitable.

Negative theology

Negative theology is what might be called a distant cousin to the theology of laughter. Essentially, it laughs at the inappropriateness of God-talk. As a rule, theologians have had a practically unlimited confidence in speaking about God, to explain and illumine the mysteries of Christian faith. The idea that faith not only seeks but can attain a rational understanding of the revealed word of God is based upon a profound confidence in our natural intellectual powers. Negative theology deflates some of this self-confidence and, in its own comical way, reminds us that because God is necessarily mysterious and ineffable, any theology or talk of God should never be taken too seriously. The living God is a hidden God. Sovereign designs and providence are impenetrable and God's ways very different from ours — so different, that they are represented as incomparable: "To whom then will you liken God, or what likeness compare with him?" (Isa. 40:18).

Negative theology is related to the theology of laughter in several ways. It exposes theology (God-talk) for what it really is: a tongue-in-cheek exercise. It laughs at the poverty and inappropriateness of human language in speaking about God and through a rapid series of negations, it shatters every conceptual limitation we may place on God. For example, we find it normal and quite fitting to call God "just." Negative theology sees something ludicrous in this idea since the distinguishing feature of justice is that a debt is acknowledged and paid. To be just means to owe something to someone and to pay that debt. But God has obligations to no one; God owes us nothing. Everything is pure gift and unsolicited grace. Thus it is equally valid to say that God is not "just" as we understand it. If we continue to insist that God is just we have attributed to God a fictitious or make-believe debt — and this, too, is quite funny when we think about it.

Negative theology is related to the theology of laughter in yet another way. Not only does it laugh at our human attempts to speak about God (and theologians are quite talkative in this regard!), but it also insists on having the last laugh. It negates its own negations, eliminating God-talk altogether. In the process of doing so it reveals an infinite darkness through which silence and love alone can discern God. In short, it teaches us that God is experienced more truthfully in the dark night and emptiness of the soul than in the most brilliant theological discourse. Today, perhaps more than at any other time in history, we need to discover this God whose pervasive and infinite love is revealed more fully in the darkness and emptiness of our life's journey. For this we need the laughter of faith more than the logic of reason. In his book, *The Deeper Life*, Louis Dupre describes the religious attitude involved in this experience of the God of darkness: "Unconditional trust without knowing what it is we trust, willingness to let go without knowing whether anyone will ever catch us, preparedness to wait without knowing whether we will be met. Total looseness and unconditional trust are the virtues negative theology teaches us to cultivate. There could be no more appropriate lesson in our time."[1] Nor could there be, I might add, a better foundation for a theology of laughter.

Negative theology, like the theology of laughter, thrives on paradox and surely the greatest paradox is faith itself. As Henri De Lubac neatly puts it: "Faith, — if it needs any support, — will often rest better on reason that resists it than on reason that appeals to it."[2] Such is the humor of faith, which grounds and justifies a theology of laughter.

Theology of play

If negative theology is a distant cousin to the theology of laughter, the theology of play can be considered its first cousin. The explosion of excellent books on the theology of play in the 1960s was hardly accidental. In human history there have certainly been times a good deal more relaxed and given to play than our own. However, no other age has had so many possibilities and occasions for play. Playgrounds and stadiums abound, video games are mass-produced, and popular sports are brought to international competitions. We Americans have an insatiable appetite for games and sports. Game-playing and fan allegiance at the college and professional levels are as American as the proverbial apple pie. It was inevitable that some form of theological reflection would emerge from our attraction for play.

The theology of play was necessary to correct our puritanical and overly solemn image of God—an image that was certainly reinforced by the old Baltimore Catechism. I remember my reaction as a young boy when told that happiness in heaven consisted in beholding God face-to-face for all eternity. "What a boring place heaven must be," I pondered and then felt a little guilty for entertaining such a sacrilegious thought. What made the prospect of heaven so grim and unattractive was the grave, cheerless image of God. The theology of play helped change such an attitude. In one of the best books on the theology of play, *Far Too Easily Pleased*, James V. Schall says, "The most difficult things to understand about God—his life, his freedom, his fascination, his relation to us—all belong to a superabundance and richness, to a freedom and attraction that make sense only if they are somehow close to what we understand as games and play."[3]

The validity of this statement hinges on the two most important characteristics of play. First, play is fundamentally linked to freedom. We play when we choose to play, and we stop playing whenever we wish. We can be compelled to work, or to sing, or to eat—but not to play. Play is characterized by free choice, more than any other form of human experience. We demonstrate freedom while at play. One only has to watch a group of children playing in a school yard to see what an affirmation of freedom play is. Even when adults play and the rules of the game are rigorously adhered to, these rules are freely accepted. Play also allows us to escape, if only for a short time, from the immediate cares and material necessities of life.

This playful freedom also characterizes God and the wonder of God's creation. God did not have to create the world, but did so—freely and for the sheer joy of it. Hugo Rahner, in his classic book on the subject, *Man at Play*, says: "When, therefore, we speak of God the creator 'playing,' there lies concealed in that phrase the metaphysical truth that the creation of the world and of man [*sic*] . . . was by no means a necessary one so far as God himself was concerned."[4]

Another important characteristic of play, and probably the most appealing one is the sense of possibility it embodies. One source of God's humor is openness to infinite possibilities. With God, anything is possible and nothing is ever repeated — literally. To encounter God means, above all, to encounter and experience unlimited possibilities as yet undreamed of, especially the possibility of becoming the person we are called to be in God's eyes. Something of the same breathtaking sense of possibility is experienced in the games we invent and play. Play is essentially an encounter with possibility. Think of the number of potential moves or game plans and strategies that are possible within the rules of a game. As Joseph Esposito and other philosophers have pointed out, in many sports it is often the player's interaction with a ball or other object difficult to control that establishes the real moment of possibility. In baseball, for example, the magic moment comes when the rim of the bat connects with the ball; in football, when a handoff or pass is attempted; in soccer, at the kick. The unpredictable bounce of the ball then creates new situations for interaction and so new possibilities. Similar moments of tantalizing possibility exist when we play with nature, as in rock-climbing, fishing, hunting, sailing, and surfing. These special moments come suddenly, often unpredictably, and with each comes the possibility of success or failure. To play, then, we must always expect the unexpected and be open to possibility. The same can be said of our encounters with God, whose infinite love is forever taking us by surprise and, if we are open to it, offering the possibility of new life.

Process Theology

A third theological development which has significant bearing on our subject is process theology. I am referring here to those scholars who developed and championed Alfred Whitehead's re-flection on God's relation to the world, such as C. Hartshorne, J.B. Cobb, Jr., Schubert Ogden, and Daniel Williams. Process theology is a radical revision of the traditional and sacrosanct idea that God is immutable (unchanging and utterly incapable of change). In the same way that playful theologies have sought to correct our overly grave and solemn image of God, process theology seeks to correct our overly static image of the Divine. The importance of this latter corrective, especially for a theology of laughter, is great. If we cannot say (in anything but a purely metaphorical sense) that God is capable or susceptible of change, then we cannot take seriously God's laughter and sense of humor and can hardly form a solid foundation for a theology of laughter.

If God is only immutable and not also mutable, if God does not change whatsoever whether creating or not creating, if we are really related to God but God not related to us, if everything we do and everything we suffer here on earth leaves God totally unaf-fected, unmoved, inert, then all our endeavors have no value. They add nothing and can add nothing to the fullness of being which is God. In short, if God can affect and influence us, but we cannot affect or influence God, then all our prayers are futile and our worship something of a sham. Certainly, the God of biblical revelation does not resemble this description.

Eulalio Baltazar presents a very readable account of process thought, which he derived from Teilhard de Chardin. In his book *God Within Process*, Baltazar situates God and the world in an evolutionary understanding of reality.[5] In this perspective, the world is more than it is now since its total reality includes its entire future, which is still in the making and in process. It is therefore necessary (in Baltazar's view) to speak of God as the never-to-be-caught-up-with-future, through which humankind and the cos-mos achieve their full reality.

Thus "becoming" or "being moved" is not seen as a weakness or an imperfection, but rather as a constitutive and metaphysical dimension of being itself. In process thought, primordial reciproc-ity exists between being and creative becoming: they are two essentially interdependent features of the same reality, much like the reciprocity that defines *father* and *son* or the reciprocity that defines *husband* and *wife*. In either instance, there is no priority of the relationship over the terms, nor of the terms over the relation. They are reciprocal. God, then, if the supreme instance of being, must also, for these words to have any coherent meaning, be the supreme instance of creative becoming.

Less abstractly, biblical revelation refers to a narrative or a "salvation history" and these terms suggest that God's innermost being is involved, affected, and moved; God does not stand aloof in Olympian immutability. God's intervention in history does indeed produce a history in God. If the Bible makes one thing thrillingly clear, it is that God is truly related to us, and that everything we do or fail to do has a real effect on God.

Already, we can see how God's laughter can be understood as real laughter, and also why his laughter, like ours, is so contagious. God is so genuinely related to us, so concerned and affected by what we do and what becomes of us, that he, too, can laugh. Indeed his laughter may be taken as an authenticating sign of his intense, dynamic, and loving relationship with us; a theological affirmation that God is so deeply in love with us that he makes himself available to us in his innermost being — he laughs.

The above theological developments form something of a family background to our theology of laughter — but only a background. To summarize, negative theology emphasizes the inappropriateness of pure rationality when speaking about God; the theology of play celebrates freedom and the surprise of unheard-of possibilities; and process theology allows God to react to, and really be affected by, what we humans do. Taken together, these correctives enhance the prospects of a theology of laughter; they even hint at what we can expect from such a theology. But before we attempt to express the deeper meaning and method of our theology (chapter 6) we must look first at the characteristically human (anthropomorphic) way the Bible speaks about God and the religious significance of such God-talk. When we say that God laughs or has a sense of humor, we are clearly in the anthropomorphic mode.

Our next task, then, is to uncover the meaning and religious significance of biblical anthropomorphism.

Endnotes

1. Louis Dupre, *The Deeper Life* (New York: Crossroad, 1981), p. 46.
2. Henri De Lubac, *Nouveaux Paradoxes* (Paris: Editions du Seuil, 1955), p. 109. (Author's translation).
3. James Schall, *Far Too Easily Pleased* (Beverly Hills, Cal.: Benziger Bruce and Glencoe, 1976), pp. 33-34.
4. Hugo Rahner, *Man at Play* (New York: Herder and Herder, 1967), p. 11.
5. Eulalio Baltazar, *God Within Process* (Paramus, N.J.: Newman Press, 1970).

The human face of divine laughter 4

*At one time, and in the Old Testament
in particular, people made free use of all
kinds of pictures, images, metaphors,
models in their talk about God.*

—Ian T. Ramsey

THEOLOGY AS A SCIENCE OF FAITH must work out its own way of speaking about God. It is concerned with an historical revelation that is accessible only in faith and has at its disposal a certain number of basic concepts related to the historical event of salvation. The task of understanding these basic concepts is, however, never complete. Whenever we speak about God our words are always inadequate; no matter how carefully we choose them, they slip, slide, and crack under the the strain. Hence, one of the permanent tasks of theology is to examine closely the way God has been spoken of in the Bible. As we take up this task, one thing becomes immediately apparent: like us, the biblical writers had to fall back on the only words at their disposal — *human* words. Not just any human words, but those especially which speak about God in a very human way.

Anyone who reads the Bible must be impressed by the frequency with which the Old Testament writers ascribe human attributes to God. God has hands, feet, eyes, ears, mouth, face, head, heart, nostrils. God uses these faculties to see, hear, speak, whistle, and eat. Yahweh's hands build, shape, create, fight, punish, write. God can walk, stroll, advance, sit, stand, and relax. Even our human reactions and feelings are not foreign to God. Yahweh laughs, gets angry, sleeps, wakes up, repents, regrets, forgets, remembers, and is jealous. What are we to make of this down-to-earth way of speaking about God? What does it mean? Before we consider the theological and religious significance of these anthropomorphic expressions, a few preliminary remarks about biblical anthropomorphism are needed. First, such anthropomorphic expressions abound in the Old Testament — from the oldest and most ancient books to the most recent. They never disappear. The psalms, the later prophets, the wisdom literature, the first apocalyptic literature, do not speak of God less realistically or more abstractly than does, say, the book of Genesis or the books of Samuel. There is evidence of some attempts to refine and tone down the more naive and exaggerated human expressions that we find in the older documents. But the biblical writers never abandon this favored mode of God-talk. Even in those documents where excessive anthropomorphic expressions have been noticeably tempered or softened (as in the priestly code and Chronicles), many other expressions are retained in spite of their obvious human connotations. Thus, for example, the biblical writers continue to speak of God's hand, house, anger, and so on. At no time do they use abstract or philosophical terms to speak of God.

These Old Testament records also lack any attempt to spiritualize such expressions by interpreting them allegorically. The tendency to allegorize came later, in post-biblical Judaism and in the Christian theology of the first centuries. A good example of this later tendency is the Jewish theologian Saadia, who wrote around the year 940 AD. "It is obvious," he says, "that what we have here are mere figures of speech, allegories: the head signifies grandeur, elevation; the eye represents providence; the ear attention; the mouth will and command; the heart is wisdom; the hand is power; the foot is subordination, submission."[1] The same allegorical interpretation can be found in Origen and in other early Christian writers. Yet this tendency to allegorize is nowhere to be found in the Old Testament—nowhere, that is, in connection with the notion or idea of God. At times some expressions are used metaphorically in a poetic vein, but they are never interpreted or explained in the arbitrary manner so common among the post-biblical writers. The Old Testament writers themselves not only refuse to abandon their anthropomorphic way of speaking about God, but they remain incurably realistic in their interpretations.

Anthropomorphism is as old as religion itself; it is found in all the religions of antiquity, from the most primitive to the most advanced. The Semitic religions, in particular, spoke in a distinctive way about their gods which certainly influenced the way the Hebrews spoke about Yahweh. The Hebrew language itself, so very concrete and realistic, also lent itself quite readily to this anthropomorphic God-talk. What concerns us here, however, is not the origin of biblical anthrpomorphism, nor the historical or linguistic factors that may have helped to shape it, but rather its theological significance.

Deceptively simple, biblical anthropomorphism reveals a powerful awareness that the God of Abraham, Isaac, and Jacob is a living God—in stark contrast to the false gods who are dead and the pagan gods who cannot speak. The difference between a living God and a lifeless idol is crucial for understanding what the biblical writers wanted to express in their human descriptions of Yahweh. The God of Israel, whose image and material representation was strictly prohibited in the Old Testament (Exod. 20:4; 20:22; Deut. 4:12; 15:18), could not possibly be represented by a lifeless image or statue. In Hebrew thought, there is an infinite difference between a plastic image and a verbal image. The former is taboo because it is a lifeless image; the latter is prized because it is a living image. Hence there is no contradiction between the abundant use of anthropomorphisms in the Old Testament, on the one hand, and the prohibition of images or sculptured representations of

Yahweh, on the other. The difference is made explicitly clear in Psalm 115:4-8.

> Their gods are made of silver and gold, formed by human hands.
> They have mouths, but cannot speak, and eyes, but cannot see.
> They have ears, but cannot hear, and noses, but cannot smell.
> They have hands, but cannot feel, and feet, but cannot walk; they cannot make a sound.
> And those who made them and who put their trust in them
> will become like the idols they have made.

The contrast here is deliberately ironic. The living God of Israel, who has hands, a mouth, eyes, and ears — like the idols — is also very unlike them in that he can act, speak, see, and hear. The concept of a living God goes to the very heart of biblical anthropomorphism. Precisely because Yahweh is a living God the Hebrews speak as one would of a living human being; and conversely, by speaking of Yahweh as a human being they continually remind themselves that their God is indeed a living God.

Yahweh is first and foremost a living and life-giving God in Hebrew faith, but also a very personal God. This second dimension of Hebrew faith is likewise powerfully expressed through biblical anthropomorphism. In fact this is where we see the tremendous difference between the Hebrew understanding of Yahweh and the Homeric understanding of the Greek gods. Both views were thoroughly anthropomorphic but in a radically different way. The fundamental purpose of Greek anthropomorphism was to picture the gods as ideal humans, and this, in the Homeric era, meant humans who were beautiful, wise, and powerful. They existed as objects of imaginative visual contemplation. They engaged in serious play with one another and with the destinies of peoples and cities.

Yahweh is completely unlike the Olympian gods. Even in the earliest traditions of the Pentateuch and the historical books of the Bible where we find the most realistic anthropomorphic expressions, there is never a suggestion about Yahweh's appearance. Indeed Hebrew faith had already determined that one could not see God and live. Yahweh's relationship to Israel, therefore, was almost entirely verbal. God commanded and promised, and, of course, kept promises. Yahweh wanted dialogue and obedience, not admiration. To those to whom he revealed himself, he was presented — not as an object for aesthetic contemplation, but as a close, personal friend or an enemy. Yahweh was not seen, but heard. God was not anthropomorphic in the sense of having a physical form, but only in the sense of being a personal subject who could speak and be spoken to, a "some-One" who could love and relate to people in the only way they could learn that they were really loved and spoken to by God.

"Living," Martin Buber says, "means being spoken to."[2] There is probably more truth in this simple statement than we realize. God seems to have thought so since his self-communication is above all a revelation through *word* — either the spoken word that physically strikes the ear, or the silent word that finds its way into the secret depths of the heart. In fact, everything in the Bible is ultimately meaningful only as the word of God: creation, election, promise, covenant, prophecy, and hope in the future. Through God's Word and this Word alone we come to know something of God's love, law, grace, and kingdom.

God speaks to us! This is without doubt the most fundamental and awesome anthropomorphism in the whole Bible. It is anthropomorphic because only humans are said to speak. It is awesome because God does indeed engage our attention and makes possible the most intimate dialogue that could exist between two partners. As R. Bultmann points out: "If theology is to avoid mere speculation about God or mere talking about the idea of God, and if it is to speak of the real living God, then it must speak of God and man [*sic*] at the same time."[3] This is the essence of biblical anthropomorphism, and it makes a theology of laughter possible.

A close look at the anthropomorphic expressions in the Bible confirms that they are all relational terms. The writers describe God in terms of what "he" does for and to his people — never in terms of what or who he is in himself. Is it not true that the human face, mouth, eye, ear, hand, arm, or foot are faculties whereby we externalize ourselves? Through them, we communicate and come into personal contact with other people; through them we can "reach out and touch someone." Only these relational human qualities are attributed to God in the Bible. Those other human features which have no such direct or obvious relational quality (bone, flesh, blood, hair, lungs, and so on), are never attributed to God. Such opaque attributes have little or no reference to our ability to communicate and relate to other people.

We see the same thing in the figures or models that represent God's activity in the Bible. Yahweh is represented as a father, mother, husband, friend, warrior, judge, shepherd, farmer, builder, potter, physician, tradesman, king, fisherman, and scribe — to mention a few. These images all refer to Yahweh's relations and dealings with his people. They too are relational and should not to be taken as descriptives of God's essence as such. Unlike the Homeric gods, the God of biblical revelation is never portrayed doing something for himself. His actions and gestures are always seen as out-going, that is, actions undertaken for — or against — his people. Even in the most anthropomorphic books of the Bible, God is never described as one who acts or does something for himself — like a man, for example, who prepares his own food, sews his own clothes, takes care of his health, builds a house, or otherwise distracts himself. The object and purpose of God's actions are always clearly and unmistakably directed to others.

In summary, the anthropomorphism of the Old Testament seeks to express the fundamental religious belief of the Hebrew community. It celebrates their lively faith in a living God, a personal God, a God who remains everlastingly in touch with his people.

To think of God with human form and qualities was justified in the Old Testament on the grounds that man and woman were created in the image of God (Gen. 1:26). In the New Testament, it is justified by the revelation of God in Jesus Christ. Indeed the mystery of the incarnation is the supreme justification of anthropomorphism. All else is but a prelude to the event of the incarnate Word, who now abandons his divine form and takes on human form (Phil. 2:7). He who previously had been described only in human terms now becomes human, "like us in all things but sin." The belief that God became human is central to Christian witness; and Christianity is set apart from all other religions by the preposterous claim: "We have heard him, we have seen him with our eyes, we have looked upon him, and our hands have touched him" (I John 1:1).

The fact that God's "hand" is now the real hand of one particular fellow human being (Jesus of Nazareth), makes the hand of every fellow human being something new—even divine. ("When you did it to one of the least of these brethren of mine, you did it to me" [Mat. 25:40].) The fact that God's "face" is now a real human face, his "word" a truly audible word, and his "heart" a real beating heart, makes every human expression of God a meaningful "sacrament." And this includes the sacrament of his divine laughter and sense of humor. Because God has a real sense of humor, every human expression of comedy and mirth is a sign of the unique smile of God contemplating his glorified Son. Thus it behooves every Christian to translate what this divine smile means for our world today.

When we imagine God laughing, this image or symbol, like so many others we have of God, can translate a genuine notion of God in an accurate way. We have many examples of such concrete and symbolic expressions in the New Testament. The "sitting at the right hand of God," for example, has a very precise and clear meaning: Christ enjoys perfect equality of nature and authority with the Most High. When our Lord says, "I am the Way," and, "I am the Door," he is in fact proclaiming his universal mediatorship. Symbolic language opens the spirit to a superabundance of truth contained in the Christian mystery, and the symbol of a laughing God is no exception.

Endnotes

1. Quoted in M. Weill, *Le judaisme*, I (Paris: Delachaux, 1866), p. 221. (Author's translation).
2. See Martin Buber, *The Knowledge of Man* (New York: Harper Torchbooks, 1965), p. 112.
3. R. Bultmann, "What sense is there to speak of God," *The Christian Scholar*, 43/3 (1960): 213-222.

God's sense of humor 5

*There was some one thing that was too
great for God to show us when he
walked upon the earth; and I have
sometimes fancied that it was his mirth.*
— G.K. Chesterton

WITH THE SURE INSTINCT and mad logic of their faith, ordinary Christians seem always to have believed, indeed believed strongly, that God has a sense of humor. Even though the writers of the synoptic gospels make no mention of Jesus ever having laughed, Christians on the whole would argue that God has a sense of humor. They might come to doubt a number of other religious truths or Church teachings, like the Pope's infallibility, the existence of angels, the exclusion of women from the priesthood. Some have even questioned the gender of God herself! But they have never wavered in their belief that God has a sense of humor. This is all the more remarkable since, as we noted earlier, there is little explicit evidence in the Bible to support such a claim, and theologians and church writers have not encouraged the idea. Not that Christians give much thought to this idea, any more than they might to the earth's being round or the sun's always setting in the west. For most Christians, God's humor is not a matter of educated awareness; rather it is something they take for granted. What lends credibility to this popular belief is that it is so spontaneously andso widely held in the absence of any authoritative or official Church teaching.

This long-standing opinion constitutes what John Cardinal Newman would have rightly regarded as the "sense of the faithful" (*sensus fidelium*), that sure instinct of the faithful people of God which allows them to perceive the truth of their faith and to discern anything that might be opposed to it. It is a deep, quasi-instinctive knowledge of the things of God, a spontaneous wisdom given by the Holy Spirit.

We know that at various times in the history of the Church this "sense of the faithful" has been judged an authentic criterion of Christian thought and devotion, especially concerning points of doctrine not yet proclaimed as revealed truths. We see this in the area of Mariology, for example, where the consensus of the faithful compensated for whatever deficiency there was in scriptural evidence or patristic testimony. The same would apply to the commonly held belief that God has a sense of humor. To confirm this, the reader has only to ask any Christian who has lived and wrestled with God over a period of years, "Does God have a sense of humor?" Nine times out of ten, the answer—quite spontaneous—will be affirmative. We might wonder how Christians came to believe this; but that they do believe it is obvious to every serious observer.

Implicit in this popular belief is the conviction that God is happy being God. Unlike humans, he always wants to be what he is, and he is what he wants to be: our Father. Maybe G.K. Chesterton was onto something after all! Maybe God's joy and laughter are just too much for us humans to cope with here on earth. Scripture tells us that "no one sees God and lives." What would happen if we experienced the full explosion or radiation of God's mirth? Alan Watts, in his whimsical little book *Beyond*

Theology, puts it this way: "If the Lord is said to veil his glory, lest it be too bright for mortal eyes, might he not also veil his mirth — perhaps as something much, much too funny for men to stand?"[1]

Notwithstanding any compassionate restraint that God may be exercising on our behalf, he does not completely hide his sense of humor from those who really love him. Christians come to know and experience it on so many different occasions: the way God writes straight with crooked lines; the funny ways he comes into our lives — usually unannounced, often surreptitiously in those awkward moments when we least wish to be disturbed; the way he foils our plans only to answer our prayers beyond our wildest dreams; the way he insists on having the last laugh whenever we take something too seriously or dismiss it too lightly; the way he plays "hide-and-seek" with us, forever disturbing us as much by his presence as by his absence; and above all the way he does impossible things with impossible people.

We usually discover God's humor through the wisdom of hindsight. Only when we look back on a particular event or circumstance in our lives do we become aware of God's humor and playfulness. The discovery is generally a delayed reaction — like that of the disciples of Emmaus who only recognized the risen Lord after he had traveled some distance with them. What prevents us from discerning and enjoying God's sense of humor more quickly and more spontaneously is not so much any self-restraint on God's part but rather our own weak faith and spiritual obtuseness.

Although Scripture makes few explicit references to God's laughter, it would be difficult to read the Bible and miss the implicit evidence of Yahweh's sense of humor. One can discern it at almost every turn of the page. "My ways are not your ways," he warns us, in one of the biggest understatements in the Bible. He takes special delight in coming into people's lives in the oddest ways, at the oddest times, making the oddest demands. We often hear that God does not expect the impossible. Yet the God of divine revelation is forever asking the impossible. He never appears bound by rules, fixed agenda, and planned encounters. He chooses the weak things of this world to confound the strong, the so-called foolish to outwit the wise; the lowly he seats ahead of the mighty. He sees in what seems rational, the irrational; in what seems important, the unimportant. Even a casual reader of the Bible is struck by the way God is forever making the truth stand on its head—like a clown!

The biblical account of salvation history reads like a succession of mind-jolting, ludicrous, disjointed happenings, and the great breakthroughs in this history have always introduced notes of dissonance. Only in retrospect do these surprise happenings add up to what we call history, that is, a sequence of events with some kind of cohesion and inner logic. This historical and typically human way of viewing salvation is largely a product of our human wisdom, our hindsight manner of describing the way God deals with us and then linking these events, like so many beads on a string, and calling the result "salvation history." In this sense, God does not "make history," nor anticipate the future as we know it. God's parenthood and love know only one law, that of the present moment. "*Now* is the acceptable time, now is the day of salvation" (2 Cor. 6:2). In a very real sense, therefore, no time is ever too soon for God, nor any time too late. We might even say that God's love and laughter are the antithesis of history; they are revealed and can only be fully appreciated at that point where the limits of history are experienced, in that most exciting, unpredictable, and free moment of our lives: the present moment, the "now" of time.

There is, then, an inherent correlation between God's existing outside of time, on the one hand, and our timely perception of God's humor on the other. It is this correlation, in fact, this surprising and incongruous wedding between time and eternity, between our human wisdom and God's divine folly, that reveals the mystery and paradox of every Christian life. When we experience the joy and the burden of this paradox, when we surrender to it, our lives and our world are never quite the same again. The experience forces us to reexamine our acquired wisdom, jars our habits of thinking about a familiar problem, and reopens judgements that had long been assumed and assimilated.

All this may seem very abstract, and that would be unfortunate since God's humor is anything but abstract. So let us take a closer look at the concrete ways God's humor is conveyed in the Bible.

Take, for example, that comical little book of Jonah, a story full of irony, surprise, and divine laughter. One of the unique features of this short work is that, unlike the other prophetic books of the Bible, it is entirely narrative. It tells the droll story of a reluctant, foot-dragging prophet who tries hard to evade God's calling and then complains bitterly to God when his feeble, unenthusiastic efforts prove to be so successful. The entire book reads like a succession of practical jokes played by God on the prophet. The singular feature of this parable lies not only in its humor, but in the distinctive kind of humor attributed to God. Here we see God's humor at its playful best, continually taking its cue from Jonah's sullen behavior, and mischievously challenging, coaxing, teasing, and outwitting the prophet only to have the last laugh. At a time when the Israelites preferred the destruction rather than the salvation of their enemies, the Lord's sense of humor turns the tables on them. Jonah succeeds in converting the people of Nineveh even when he is not really trying. The true irony, of course, is that God's love, even when disguised as sheer folly, proves irresistible and affirms the absolute right of the beloved to exist.

God's tongue-in-cheek humor is present everywhere in the Bible. We recognize this humor immediately if we remember it generally goes against our most logical judgements. It turns some of our biggest ambitions in life into shattered dreams and our biggest blunders into blessings. Frederick Buechner captures this comic vision in his book *Telling the Truth*. Biblical scholars will undoubtedly take exception to Buechner's light-hearted exegesis, but then, biblical studies are not particularly noted for their humor.

> Who could have predicted that God would choose,
> not the honest and reliable Esau, but Jacob, the
> trickster and heel? Who would have dreamed that he
> would put the finger on Noah, who hit the bottle, or
> on the prophets, who were a ragged lot, mad as

hatters most of them, always dragging their heels
when they were called to hit the sawdust trail? Who
could have foretold that out of the sordid affair
between David and Uriah's wife, Bathsheba,
Solomon would be born with his high IQ and his
passion for ecclesiastical architecture? Who could
have guessed that out of Solomon would be born a
whole line of apostate kings, ending finally in a king
the likes of whom nobody could have foretold . . .[2]

Indeed, with the dramatic events of the Incarnation we see the
irresistible folly and humor of God. Here we are given, as never
before, the assurance that it is all right to laugh. The Incarnation is
a comedy of grace because no one expected salvation to come from
"within" humankind, that is, from the very dust, the clay, and the
mud with which we earthbound creatures are so familiar. The
Savior was expected to come from "on high" with power and
might, as befits any heavenly king, not as a helpless, shivering babe
lying in a manger. Can anything be quite so funny? What cannot
possibly happen does indeed happen, and it happens in the dark
that just barely fails to swallow it up. The comedy of grace in all this
is, of course, that this world for all its ugliness and this body for all
its frailties and this time for all its mad logic are precisely where
God wants to be.

This comic grace is carried through into the life and teaching
of Jesus. As Conrad Hyers summarizes it:

The "sinless" are invited to cast the first stone.
Those with logs in their eyes are cautioned about
trying to take out specks of dust in other people's
eyes. Scribes and Pharisees are passed over in favor
of publicans and sinners. . . . The most despised man
in the village is invited to have tea with the Messiah.
Jesus as a Jew asks water of a Samaritan woman of
doubtful repute. Even small children are said to be
closer to the Kingdom of God than Jesus' own
disciples. And the King of the Jews is welcomed into

Jerusalem riding on a donkey, and given a cross for a
throne and thorns for a crown.[3]

What divine foolishness! And yet the best was still to come.
There would be another burst of cosmic humor, even more
unforeseeable, when another angel on another occasion announced
to a disbelieving world the biggest practical joke of all, "He is risen,
he is not here" (Matt 28:6).

Why is it, then, that God's mirth and laughter have not been
celebrated and given more prominence in organized religion,
especially in the Church's liturgical rites and pastoral approach? Is
it not strange that religion is so somber and God so mirthful? The
majority of practicing Christians know that God has a sense of
humor, that divine blessings often come in the most ludicrous way.
They know this from personal experience, and in the fact that they
can continue to trust God despite so many negative trends and
tragedies around them. Yet the Church as an institution, as an
organized religion, does not reflect this faith experience of its
members. Church leaders, who set its rules and preside over its life,
seem unaware of God's mirth—not opposed to it, not trying to
undermine it, just invincibly ignorant of it. If we are to speak of
church renewal—as we must—this is one area where it is long
overdue. The discrepancy between what the Church does and
teaches officially, on the one hand, and what its members believe
privately, on the other, has always been a signal and call for renewal.

My contention throughout this study is that the Christian
God can indeed laugh as heartily as any Homeric or Canaanite
god—only more so! While organized religion has not made suf-
ficient allowance for God's mirth, the faithful themselves should be
encouraged to pursue their quest for the source and author of all
laughter. They at least have heard some distant echoes of this
heavenly laughter. They can also take comfort that the idea of a
laughing God is not altogether absent from our Christian tradition
(provided that one looks hard enough).

Meister Eckhart, the celebrated fourteenth century scholastic,
was one who believed that God laughs out of an abundance of

divine life, energy, and love. He tells us we should never put our trust in a spirituality that is devoid of laughter, because good humor and laughter characterize the innermost relations between the persons of the Trinity. "When the Father laughs to the Son," he says, "and the Son laughs back to the Father, that laughter gives pleasure, that pleasure gives joy, that joy gives love, and love gives the persons of which the Holy Spirit is one."[4] Eckhart's God is a God who rejoices—a pleasurable, joyful, laughing God. If God laughs everlastingly, it is not because he is remote, sovereign, or inaccessible. Nor is it because he is uncaring and indifferent to what happens here on earth. God's laughter is a sign of love, full of tender persuasion. For Eckhart, God's laughter is as great as his love, and his love is full of sheer delight and laughter.

Christians know that God has a sense of humor, not from reading the Bible, but by reflecting on their lives. There is something about the way God loves us, something inherently funny, that gives us an experiential knowledge of his divine humor. God's loving advances enable us to understand why there is so much to laugh about in these privileged moments of grace. In order to understand how Christians come to know God's sense of humor, we must turn to their personal experience of his love. The correlation between God's love and God's humor is found in what might be called his tremendous "sense of possibility." One of the recurrent images attributed to God in the Bible is the ability to "change his mind," to have "second thoughts," to "relent"—in short, the ability to reverse an earlier decision in favor of something new. This human way of depicting God is not just a metaphor or a poetic figure of speech. It points to a deeper and more fundamental religious truth about God's love, namely, his acute "sense of possibility." With God all things are possible (Matt. 12:26), and the believer knows this statement means things could just as easily be otherwise. This possibility makes God and everything he does so humorous. This is why God can laugh. He knows that anything and everything could just as easily be different. God laughs at the unlimited possibilities that divine love is forever opening up for us, possibilities so real for us that we call them the Kingdom of God.

God's comic spirit is revealed in the possibility that we might become perfect as God is perfect, that even the rich are impossibly saved in the end just as a camel somehow impossibly makes it through the eye of a needle, and that God's will can be done on earth as it is in heaven. We are even asked to envisage the real possibility of a new heaven and a new earth. Heard as a wonderful joke — preposterous and ringing with divine laughter — we know it to be true. John Donne says that "God is wild" and John the Apostle states that "God is love." When Christians make the connection between the two, when they discover just how wild God's love really is, they come to know something of his incredible humor.

God's infinite patience also reveals another humorous aspect of God's love. At no time are we more certain that God has a sense of humor than in those grace-filled moments when we realize that God tolerates our bungling performance and repeated failures with much greater patience than we do. This knowledge always comes as a comic surprise to us because it comes when we get discouraged with ourselves (what Søren Kierkegaard calls the "despair of weakness"). It comes when we no longer desire or expect to achieve anything great or good in life, when reality for us comes to mean a dull acceptance of the amenities of life, emptied of every enthusiasm. In short, it comes at those joyless and irritable moments which require great effort to remember that we were once able to laugh at ourselves. At such times God's patience takes us by surprise and reveals its good humor. Suddenly, we realize that God does have a comic spirit after all: he still loves us.

When we become a fearful burden to ourselves, God's patience gives him the last laugh. He is always ready to forgive us, however undeserving we may be; always ready to be patient with us, however unreasonable we may be; always ready to explore new possibilities, however unteachable we may be. God is funny because of the outlandish risks he is prepared to take on our behalf. He knows that his love for us may, at any time, be cheated, betrayed, tormented, or worse still, ignored. Yet God is patient and forever eager to take that risk, and so a Christian can know God's humor and begin to hear an echo of God's heavenly laughter.

Imagine what might happen if God's laughter became a living religious symbol in the Church, just as God's anger or God's omnipotence or God's providence once were. Since the truth and reality of God's sense of humor is already inchoately present in the hearts of the faithful, the symbol of a laughing God would not be an artificial contrivance or an afterthought. Rather it would correspond to a truth about God which most Christians already existentially sense. Lived and experienced as a religious symbol, God's laughter would become much more vibrant than a mere intellectual idea or a fleeting awareness; it would engage the believer's whole being, affecting the person's attitudes and behavior at the deepest level of faith.

More specifically, such a living symbol would open our eyes to the central manifestation of God's comical freedom in love which has gained a resounding victory over all the forces that fracture our unity, cause us anxiety, and imprison our spirit. The symbol of a laughing God would dispel many of our unnecessary fears and would free us from the inhuman pressure of constantly having to prove ourselves. It would set us free, without making us passive, for a more inwardly relaxed, cheerful, and truly Christian life.

The proper function of any religious symbol is not to insert God's activity into the world or into the ordinary course of our lives, as though God were absent from us and our world. Rather its function is to make us even more keenly aware of God's presence in our world and what it might mean if we set out in all possible haste to be there with him. The symbol of a laughing God would direct our attention to the fact that life is more hope-filled than we ordinarily conceive it to be, that the human condition, even the most wretched, has within it the promise of redemption and ultimate liberation. It would set us within an ecclesial setting where the foibles and profound discrepancies of life are consciously brought to our attention and put in perspective. It would keep alive for us that carefree spirit so typical of God and little children, that joyous buoyancy of "letting go" even in the face of those seemingly rock-like necessities of life. Then perhaps we might understand what our Lord meant when he spoke of the "birds of the air" and the "lilies of the field," and why with that sense of humor, God allows powerlessness to become the model of power and folly, an example of God's wisdom (I Cor. 7:17-31).

Endnotes

1. Alan Watts, *Beyond Theology* (New York: Pantheon Books, 1964), p. 56.
2. Frederick Buechner, *Telling the Truth* (New York: Harper and Row, 1977), pp. 57-58.
3. Conrad Hyers, "The Comic Vision in a Tragic World," *The Christian Century* (April 20, 1983): 366-367.
4. Raymond B. Blakney, *Meister Eckhart: A Modern Translation* (New York: Harper Torchbooks, 1941), p. 245.

A theology of laughter   6

*Laughter has something in it in
common with the ancient winds of faith
and inspiration . . . it makes people
forget themselves in the presence of
something greater than themselves;
something (as the common phrase goes
about a joke) that they cannot resist.*
— G.K. Chesterton

A CLUE TO THE THEOLOGICAL MEANING of laughter lies in
remembering how we learned to ride a bicycle. No one muscle,
grip, or way of leaning could get us started or keep us balanced and
riding. Nor were verbal instructions very helpful; as novices we
were perhaps even irritated when someone told us to lean into the
turn or to keep peddling even as the bike was beginning to topple.
Concentrating too much on any particular aspect could jeopardize
a precarious balance. Success happens when the separate physical
skills and muscular exertions all come together. The particulars of
vision, leaning, peddling, holding on, and turning, are suddenly
unified in a single whole and this "sudden glory" gives meaning to
each unspoken part. In fact, the thrill of riding comes from feeling
something new emerge in the combination of many ordinary and
dull particulars.

So it is with the theology of laughter. As we have already seen, there are many elements that constitute humor and provoke laughter; surprise, unpredictability, contrast, incongruity, possibility. None of these, however, has much religious meaning in itself. But when they come together, when these separate elements coalesce in such a way as to, make sense within the context of faith, they become pregnant with meaning. In this religious experience a thrilling new something emerges, the sudden awareness of God's liberating sense of humor. At first, it may be only a larval religious intimation; but it has become with many saints a full-fledged spirituality. Hence, a theology of laughter becomes not only possible but feasible.

The principle aim of theology is to understand the faith of Christians, and to work out in a way that is intellectually exact, communicable, and verifiable, the message which in faith is believed to be true. Theology follows, registers, and clarifies what the faithful believe; it tries to "explain" this living faith in a way that unfolds its richness and reveals its organic unity. Theology must always be grounded in the common experience of the Christian community; so our theology of laughter is grounded in the Christian consensus that God has a sense of humor. As we have already noted, this remarkable affirmation of faith is not the fruit of explicit reasoning, but rather an immediate and intuitive recognition in the Spirit. This belief is the starting point, the larval stage, of our theology of laughter. What follows is nothing but the methodical and critical unfolding of this Christian consensus. Our theology of laughter probes the density of this belief and uncovers its richness and theological meaning.

The invisible hand of God

One of the more obvious meanings implied in the Christian's affirmation of God's humor is that God has a providential finger even in chance events. We are all familiar with what is commonly referred to as a chance encounter, a lucky break, a fluke of science, or a trick of fate. The dictionary defines chance as an event for which there is no apparent cause or rational explanation, the absence of any known reason why an event should turn out one way rather than another. Christians feel uncomfortable with this definition because in the context of faith nothing ever really happens by pure chance. No event in world history or in private life is believed to be totally meaningless. What at first appears as fortuitous, in hindsight is usually seen as providential. A Christian will scrutinize these so-called chance events or blind spots in life and try to discover the invisible hand of God, "the hint half-guessed, the gift half-understood" in them. The English physician and author, Sir Thomas Browne, puts it this way: "Surely there are in everyone's life certain contradictions, twists, and turns which pass awhile under the category of chance, but at the last, well examined, prove to be the very hand of God."[1]

A classical example of this turn of events is the fortuitous (read "providential") way a certain reading of Cicero became instrumental in St. Augustine's conversion. He writes in his *Confessions*:

> That particular book is called *Hortensius* and contains
> an exhortation to philosophy. Quite definitely it
> changed the direction of my mind, altered my
> prayers to you, O Lord, and gave me a new purpose
> and ambition. Suddenly all the vanity I had hoped in
> I saw as worthless, and with an incredible intensity
> of desire I longed after immortal wisdom. I had
> begun that journey which was to lead to you.[2]

C. S. Lewis is another who experienced God's humor in his life and even entitled his autobiography *Surprised by Joy*. God broke into Lewis' life in the usual way: unexpectedly, unpredictably, and seemingly by chance. In Lewis' case the surprise came by means of nature, or as he himself says, "what I can only describe as the Idea of Autumn."[3]

This is Christian hindsight at its best; the realization that "all is grace" and that even a chance reading of a book or a chance encounter with nature can be an instrument through which God touches the depths of a person's soul. This discovery is what makes a Christian laugh deep down inside: the interesting, beautiful, splendid aspect of God's humor in its character of surprise, of unexpected and sudden revelation. The whole affair, though divine, suddenly seems as natural and common as riding a bicycle. What really makes a Christian want to laugh is knowing that these surprising grace-filled results hang so precariously on what is surely a very common human occurrence (reading a book, looking at a sunset). The results are also funny because God's grace is predestined and yet freely accepted, that is, both unavoidable and avoidable. One reason St. Augustine could never come to terms with the mystery of predestination and human freedom, I suspect, is because in his dogmatics he failed to take sufficiently into account God's sense of humor. Hans Urs von Balthasar is absolutely right when he says that "dogmatics can only be written with and through humor."

We say that a person has a sense of humor if he or she can "see through something." This is precisely what a theology of laughter tries to do, to "see through" the many paradoxes that surround our lives and in the tangle of historical events discern the folly of God's humor and the direction of God's love.

The sanctification of trivia

However, the theology of laughter is not only hindsight theology. While after-the-fact appreciation of God's practical jokes is always taken into account, another dimension must be considered: God's humor is also experienced as a present reality, especially in the daily routine of our "everyday" lives.

According to Cicero, "The gods attend to great matters and neglect small ones." While this may be so in Roman mythology, nothing could be farther from the truth with regard to the God of biblical revelation. The Bible makes clear nothing is small or trite in the eyes of God: "Indeed the very hairs on your head are numbered" (Luke 12:7). It might even be said that the smaller a thing is, the more God seems to prize and value it. Herein lies one of the secrets of God's sense of humor.

A great Judaic theologian of our time, Abraham Heschel, calls attention to this concept in the Old Testament. In his book *Man is Not Alone*, he says: "The Bible insists that God is concerned with everydayness, with the trivialities of life. The great challenge does not lie in organizing solemn demonstrations, but in how we manage the commonplace ... .The predominant feature of the biblical pattern of life is unassuming, unheroic, inconspicuous piety, the sanctification of trifles, attentiveness to details."[4]

In the New Testament, God's attentiveness to and concern for smallness is even more manifest—beginning with the amazing way God's son chose to come into our world: "And the shepherds came in haste and found their way to Mary and Joseph, and the infant cradled in a manger" (Luke 2:16). Our Lord often spoke solicitously about "the little ones" (meaning ordinary people in the broadest sense, the poor, uneducated, socially inferior). He also constantly referred to "smallness" as a privileged point of comparison.

A few examples follow:

- "The kingdom of heaven is like a mustard seed ... the tiniest of all seeds" (Matt. 13:31).
- "He who is faithful in small things is faithful in big things also" (Luke 16:10).
- "He who is the least among you all is the greatest" (Luke 9:48).
- "Whoever makes little of himself like this little child is the greatest in the kingdom of heaven" (Matt. 18:4).
- "Let the children alone, and do not stop them from coming to me. The kingdom of heaven belongs to such as these" (Matt. 19:14).
- "Whoever gives only a refreshing drink to one of these little ones ... will not go without his reward" (Matt. 10:42).
- "Inasmuch as you did this to one of these least brethren of mine, you did it to me" (Matt. 26:40).

- "Take care you do not despise any one of these little ones" (Matt.18:10).
- "I praise you, Father, Lord of heaven and earth, for hiding these things from the wise and prudent and revealing them to little ones. Yes, Father, for such has been your good pleasure" (Luke 10:21).

Can there be any doubt that in the eyes of God "small is eternally beautiful?" Many of the great saints thought so, like Francis of Assisi, Philip Neri, Therese of Lisieux with her doctrine of the "little way," and the English mystic, Julian of Norwich, to whom God revealed his infinite love, as she says, "in a little thing, no bigger than a hazelnut."

Indeed it is safe to say that Christians of every age have discovered God's humor more in the concealed dignity of small things than in great or spectacular ones. This is not surprising. The richest store of divine humor is always found right in our own backyard, at the heart of our daily routine and everyday cares. It is in the wretched humdrum of our daily preoccupations, in the gray tedium of dull routine, amid all that is commonplace and insignificant, that Christians are most apt to sense the presence of God's humor. In these tedious hours when our lives seem so ordinary, so empty of anything great, God reveals a most exquisite sense of humor to those who love and believe in him.

Things never seem much bigger than a hazelnut in my daily routine and yet any one segment of it, even the smallest or the most insignificant, can suddenly become "full of grace." Put your finger down anywhere, and you touch something that can become holy, sacramental, something that participates in the Incarnation and relates to the kingdom of heaven. For example, the prospect of meeting and recognizing Christ—of all places!—in our neighbor. The humor of faith encourages such divine recognition and makes us laugh, because in most cases only a "fool" could possibly see the "real presence" of Christ in this particular neighbor. So the joke is invariably on us and without thinking too much about it we have become, as Paul says, "fools for Christ's sake" (1 Cor. 4:10). We laugh because the sacrament of the neighbor is so available, so ordinary, and at the same time so exalted. We laugh also because if it does turn out to be true in the end—that Christ *is* in our neighbor, as Matthew describes in his gospel (25:31-40), then we will really have something to laugh about. Which bring us to another aspect of the theology of laughter, namely, its future-oriented humor.

The perception of possibility

"Faith is the assurance of things hoped for, the conviction of things we cannot see," says the author of Hebrews. The theology of laughter interprets this statement to mean that a Christian is one who has a wild imagination and a fantastic sense of possibility—that special grace to believe that "things could just as easily be different from what they are." For a true believer, Christian hope places no restrictions and knows no bounds. Indeed Christians have often been known to "hope against hope" (Rom. 8:18). In the discrepancy between what actually is, on the one hand, and what could possibly be, on the other, God's humor appears. The sharper the discrepancy, and the more sudden the perception of it, the more humorous the matter becomes.

Laughter is the perception of possibility, and this includes the possibility that miracles do happen. Every Christian is familiar with the gospel episode in which Jesus walked on the water to rejoin his distressed disciples. The religious meaning of this story is obvious. The Lord will go to any length to be reunited with his followers when they are in difficulty; nothing can keep him from them. Our Christian sense of possibility, and therefore our humor, is grounded in this conviction, that if need be Christ can again walk on water and pass through closed doors (John 20:19), that his hand is not too short to save (Is. 59:1) — in brief, that anything is possible with God (Luke 1:37).

Nowhere is this eschatological aspect of God's humor better revealed than when a Christian or a Christian community is at prayer. Do we not see divine comedy at its best when Christian prayer boldly asks for the "impossible" in the name of the Lord Jesus? For example, when a mother prays for the recovery of her terminally ill child; when a Christian prays for any lost cause or hopeless case, or for the dead, in the firm belief that such prayers can and do make a difference; when a Christian offers up to God his or her own physical sufferings and thinks that this will "make up what is still lacking in Christ's sufferings" (Col. 1:24) — as though something were indeed lacking; or when any Christian fights against overwhelming odds (as did David against Goliath) and, through prayer, affirms the possibility of peace and justice in a world gone mad.

In every such case, the living tradition of the "holy fool" lives on in the Church. Indeed it is the vocation of all Christians, especially those who have experienced God's humor in their personal lives. Perhaps this attitude explains why authentic Christianity must always seem like madness to the world. Yet the real purpose of prayer, even when asking for the impossible, is to give God a chance to convince us that we have indeed been heard, that what lies in the depths of our hearts is understood. We pray so that God's sense of humor becomes contagious and prepares us to accept the divine will. Whatever the final outcome of our impossible prayers, we want to be able to laugh "with him and in him."

In this way, then, Christians generally come to experience and believe in God's sense of humor and mirth. Our theology of laughter is only an attempt to monitor, explain, and express this faith experience. To give an intellectually honest account of Christian laughter three elements have emerged in our elaboration of this theology: the invisible hand of God, the sanctification of trivia, and the perception of possibility. Taken together, these elements constitute what might be called the foundations of Christian laughter. Put in a slightly different way, this spiritual tripod is what makes a Christian want to laugh. Whether or not an audible burst of laughter materializes is another question; but the urge to laugh is real because the believer's faith is real. What prompts a Christian to laugh is the liberating perception that God is already laughing, and God's laughter, like his love, is contagious; it makes us want to laugh. Our laughter of faith, therefore, is always contingent upon God: it is an echo, an aftereffect, of God's own initial mirth and unsolicited humor. In short, we laugh *because* God laughs first.

It remains to be seen how this theology finds practical application in our daily life of faith and ministry. But we must first turn our attention to those qualities which distinguish Christian laughter from ordinary profane laughter.

Endnotes

1. Sir Thomas Brown, *Religio Medici: The Norton Anthology of English Literature*, vol. I (New York: W.W. Norton, 1968), p. 1237.
2. St. Augustine, *Confessions*, trans. F.J. Sheed (New York: Sheed and Ward, 1943), p. 45.
3. C. S. Lewis, *Surprised by Joy* (New York: Harcourt, Brace and World, 1955), pp. 16-17.
4. Abraham Heschel, *The Insecurity of Freedom* (New York: Schocken Books, 1972), pp. 102-103.

Christian or profane?　　7

*Religion gives the comic all its
significance and justifies laughter.*
— Peter Berger

*The inner essence of humor lies, no
matter how heretical this may seem, in
the strength of one's religious disposition.*
— P. Lersch

WILLIAM L. SULLIVAN ONCE SAID that the first curse which the Almighty puts on those who deny him is to deprive them of their sense of humor. Whether or not this is true, one thing seems certain: those who love and serve the Lord come to know something of God's infectious sense of humor. Indeed the freshest type of humor, the humor of saints, knows instinctively that all parenthood, all love, and all laughter come from God. Saints have a keen sense of humor because they see through the eyes of God who sees through everything. In one form or other, humor is one of the hallmarks of the truly spiritual person. It presupposes, as we shall see, a detachment, a real passion for life and everything that breathes life, a tongue-in-cheek familiarity with God, and an uncommon courage in the face of adversity and injustice. Whenever we find Christians seriously bent on following Christ, we hear the echo of heavenly laughter. For it is generally at the heart of one's Christian existence that the relaxed intensity of God's humor is revealed and makes all things appear in a new light.

Many saints, especially in the Holy Fools tradition of past centuries, went out of their way to become "fools for Christ's sake" (1 Cor. 4:10), with a type of holiness that went against the conventional standards of proper behavior. Through a holy madness, feigned or real, they devoted themselves entirely to the service of God by accepting voluntarily the role of a fool or village idiot. They made themselves ridiculous in both appearance and behavior in order to teach people the truth of Christ and to speak this truth openly to the powerful of their day.

The name of St. Francis of Assisi readily comes to mind as one who successfully carried this foolish tradition into the Middle Ages. There was about him, as Chesterton puts it, "something of gentle mockery at the very idea of possessions, something of a hope of disarming the enemy by generosity, something of a humorous sense of bewildering the worldly with the unexpected, something of the joy of carrying an enthusiastic conviction to a logical extreme."[1]

In more recent times, and in keeping with this tradition, we have witnessed a revival of this spirituality with the explicit representation of Christ as a clown in the paintings of Georges Rouault, in musicals like *Godspell*, in movies like *The Parable* and *A Clown is Born*, and in the resurgence of Christian clowning as a full-time ministry. The point I wish to stress here is that Christian laughter, as in so many other aspects of our spirituality, will often appear inappropriate or excessive in the eyes of the world. It is certainly not something that one learns, say, at an Emily Post summer camp. To many, Christian laughter will appear as "reason made mischievous" — or worse still "reason gone mad." Therefore we need serious discernment.

Laughter is not Christian simply because the person who does the laughing happens to be a Christian. Nor does it follow that Christians have an exclusive monopoly on holy laughter. We also know that laughter shares in the very ambiguity of human existence. It can be either the concrete embodiment of worldly cynicism or it can be a sign of God's presence; it can be holy or sinful, liberating or oppressive, creative or destructive—in short, a process of liberation or imprisonment. So at what point is laughter more than mere human laughter? When is ordinary laughter truly Christian? In the concrete, historical circumstances in which we live, it is not easy to distinguish between holy laughter and worldly laughter, partly because on the surface there is little or no difference between the two. Laughter may be transparent, but it rarely discloses the spirit which prompts or provokes it. In this area, as in all spiritual matters, the discernment of spirits is important. We know that the Holy Spirit "breathes where it will"—sometimes as a sudden, unpredictable impulse; at other times as a gentle, unobtrusive, and scarcely perceptible urge. While these inner promptings of the Spirit do come from beyond the human faculties and powers, beyond the modalities of the human psyche, they nevertheless manifest themselves in and through human means. They become incarnate, shrouded in the veil of human ambiguity.

In order to understand what makes Christians laugh and why their humor is so special, we must look deeper into the subsoil of Christian life. Every authentic life has a ground from which it springs and in which it is always rooted. Christian laughter is no exception. It takes its origin in the hidden depths of our life in Christ. What follows, therefore, is an attempt to offer a few criteria (by no means all) for discerning genuine Christian laughter. This reflection should help us to know when a person is provoked into laughter by nothing less exciting than the Spirit of the living God. I hope it will also provide a theologically sound basis for a genuine spirituality of Christian humor.

Sign #1: Detachment

The first and perhaps most fundamental criterion is reflected in our Lord's statement to all his would-be followers: "If anyone comes to me, and does not hate his own father and mother and wife and children and brothers and sisters, yes, even his own life, he cannot be my disciple" (Luke 14:26). This text is one of the strongest, most beautiful, and most embarrassing in the Gospel. Properly understood, it explains many things in the lives of Christians, including their peculiar sense of humor. Jesus is not asking for hate, but for total detachment. This detachment is a basic independence toward all that is not God, an authentic readiness and availability for anything that God could ask (see Luke 9:57-62).

Granted that Christians are involved in their immediate environment, as Christ certainly was. But every sentence of the Gospel shows that he was by no means absorbed in it. One cannot fail to see that Jesus is fully a part of the real world of his day, while observing that he is also singularly detached from it. He is very much "of his time yet outside it." Those who encountered him were disturbed, puzzled, and often startled by his strange detachment—including his family circle, his relatives, and his disciples. Perhaps more surprising still, a strong note of detachment is visible in his relationship with his mother (see Luke 2:49; John 2:4; Mark 3:31-35; Luke 11:28). So the pattern of Christ's life, which has always been the most authenticating norm against which Christians shape their own lives, includes an uncommon degree of detachment.

There can be no real Christian laughter without the inner freedom that comes with detachment. In fact, this spiritual distancing is what gives Christians the ability to transcend the narrow limits of their immediate environment and see the larger picture. They are not caught in the parochial worship of that culture in which they are born, and so they can laugh at their own society from the standpoint of the Gospel. Christians know that no matter how much importance is given to personal and national power, wealth and security, these values cannot be taken with ultimate seriousness. Christian laughter is the sign of a mind at peace with itself, a humble recognition of the relativity of all finite perspectives.

There is such a close connection between detachment and Christian humor that a decline in one usually means a decline in the other. Without the detachment of humor or the humor of detachment, it is doubtful whether the paradoxes of Christian life can be fully embraced and acted upon: a life that is rooted in the eternity of God as well as in the dust and muddiness of the world, a life of pitiable misery and breathtaking greatness, a life charged with the resounding victory of Christ as well as with the sorry relapses of human frailty. Without the comic flair of detachment, it is difficult to see how we can meet the demands of the Gospel: to be in the world yet not of the world, to be wise as serpents yet meek as doves, to pray as though everything depended on God and yet feed the hungry as though everything depended on us, to lose our life in order to save it, to pardon unpardonable sins and love unlovable people.

The whole thrust of Jesus' proclamation, which Christian laughter keeps alive in the world, is a challenge to conceive the inconceivable, to say what cannot be said, to applaud what should not be applauded, and to do what cannot be done. Christian laughter interprets Jesus' parables in the modern world as Jesus did, by jarring and overturning prior judgments, closed options, and fixed conclusions. It summons the world to recognize in the reversal of human judgments and human situations a sign that the Kingdom of God is truly at hand and in our midst (Luke 17:21).

Sign #2: Reverence for life

Another criterion which may be helpful in judging the authenticity of Christian laughter is a deep reverence for life. Laughter is Christian when it makes life grow, expand, and develop; it is not Christian when it attempts to strangle, suppress, and destroy life. Beneath all Christian laughter is a bold affirmation of life, a conviction that the God of biblical revelation is a living and life-loving God. Not only does God preserve and protect life (Ps. 66:9), but Christ came, as John says, that we might have life and have it in abundance (John 10:10). If Jesus came to bring us richer and more abundant life, then surely our laughter ought to be richer and more abundant. If it is not, the fault does not lie in Christ's unexpected Good News, but in our own fear and refusal to take him seriously, a refusal to believe that when Jesus said "life" he really meant life.

The intrinsic connection between life and laughter is powerfully expressed in a play by Eugene O'Neill, called *Lazarus Laughed*. The play deals with Lazarus' life after Jesus summoned him from the grave. It is the story of Jesus' friend who has tasted death and sees it for what it is, a man whose constant refrain is to invite others to join him in laughter:

> Laugh with me!
> Death is dead!
> Fear is no more!
> There is only life!
> There is only laughter![2]

O'Neill tells us: Lazarus "begins to laugh, softly at first," then heartily, "a laugh so full of a complete acceptance of life, a profound assertion of joy in living, so devoid of all fear, that it is infectious with love," so infectious that, despite themselves, his listeners are caught up by it and carried away.

This infectiousness is the hallmark of Christian laughter. It is not that we blind ourselves to sin and war and disease and death. These tragedies will touch us just as cruelly as they touch the man or woman who does not believe, who cannot hope, who refuses to love. But we can still laugh and find joy in life. Why? Because in the midst of death we know and believe that God keeps every promise. If the God we believe brought life where death had seemed invincible in the experience of Christ, then we are free to look for life in the most threatening moments of our lives and our world. Nothing of significance can ever be said of Christian laughter that does not stem from Christ's victory over death.

We sing and laugh this faith in many ways, but Psalm 126 is a good script. In this psalm it is obvious that evil times had fallen upon God's people shortly after their return from exile; drought, locusts, and a poor harvest had reduced the community to poverty. Yet in spite of everything, they maintained a trusting hope in their God, who always and continually restored his people, as much by his presence as by his promise. It was this hope, this prospect of a better life, that made them laugh. Not only were they able to laugh, but they surrendered themselves to unrestrained delight, their mouths filled with laughter and their lips with song.

Such is the humor of hope. It enables us to laugh at the prospect of life when others see only cause for despair. It is a laughter that rolls back the stones of empty tombs and reveals the resurrection. It is a laughter that loves the world with the eyes of those who are not yet born.

Sign #3: Familiarity with God

If Christian laughter originates in the paradox of detachment, and thrives on a deep reverence for life, it is ultimately provoked by a tongue-in-cheek familiarity with God, best expressed in Jesus' words: "You are my friends" (John 15:15). Christian laughter registers both the abyss that separates us from God and the closeness and familiarity we enjoy with God in Christ. We laugh because we know how far we fall short of the measure of God and yet are called friends. When the mad logic of this divine love strikes home, as it invariably will with every sincere Christian, we laugh, like Sarah, because we suddenly realize there must have been a mistake. We laugh all the more when we remember that Christ always had a predilection for the poor, the outcast, the unworthy, and the insignificant. Friendship with little ones has always been a sign of God's sense of humor. So it strikes us as very funny that we, too, should be numbered among "the least" and "the lost."

Add to this the fact that many of us were born into a Christian family and home, and thus were "automatically" baptized into God's close friendship and table fellowship. Then we have even more reason to laugh because our friendship with God seems to have been "inherited" from our parents or grandparents, much like our blue eyes or brown hair. It came to us so naturally that we can truly call it our very own; yet it remains one of the greatest graces God can bestow. The divine humor in all this is the fact that even those supernatural and unthinkable gifts that God alone can grant are given to us as though we had given them to ourselves—not willfully, but seemingly by chance. This divine folly strikes laughter in the heart of every Christian who, in the silence of his or her conscience, asks: "Why me?" So we laugh, as Lazarus did, and in our tears of joy and laughter we are reminded of W.H. Auden's words in "For the Time Being":

> Therefore, see without looking, hear without
> listening, breathe without asking:
> The Inevitable is what will seem to happen to you
> purely by chance;
> The Real is what will strike you as really absurd;
> Unless you are certain you are dreaming, it is certainly a dream of your own;
> Unless you exclaim—"There must be some mistake"
> —you must be mistaken.[3]

So we laugh because God is close to us, closer to us, in fact, than we are to ourselves. In God, as Paul says, we live and move and have our whole being. Yet our comic predicament is real. We are at once close to God and yet seemingly so distant. In his remarkable essay *The Dialectic of the Sacred and the Comic*, Conrad Hyers says: "Just as the more serious reaction to the sacred is one of both shrinking back and drawing close, like the movement of the moth around the flame, so the comic response to the sacred is both withdrawing and aggressive."[4] Laughter shares this holy ambivalence with all sacred mysteries; it is at once terrible and fascinating.[5] In our close encounters with God, we want to distance and separate ourselves, on the one hand, like Simon Peter who cried out: "Depart from me, O Lord, for I am a sinful man" (Luke 5:8); on the other hand, we are just as bold in our desire to be intimate with God as were the disciples of Emmaus who invited the Lord: "Stay with us, for it is nearly evening and the day is almost over" (Luke 24:29).

A curious dilemma characteristic of every faith commitment confronts us here. We must love and serve God with all our heart, but we must also be aware that it will probably cost us our lives. Abraham epitomizes for believers this awkward predicament when he was commanded by God to take his beloved child Isaac to Moriah and offer him there as a burnt offering (Gen. 22:2). Familiarity with God invariably puts us in a similar existential predicament. Anyone who is a Christian, who follows Christ and enjoys table fellowship with him, knows this experience. Only through the laughter of faith, the laughter of one who appears to be out of his or her mind, is the dilemma overcome and an Abraham-like obedience is made possible.

To illustrate this dilemma, I would like to conclude with a personal example from my own experience of priestly celibacy.

Ever since I was young, I wanted to become a priest. Yet there was never a time that I did not want a wife and a family of my own. Hence the tension of so many who feel called to the priesthood. We are all familiar with the arguments for and against celibate priest-hood, but the dilemma remains real. Whatever else may be said about priestly celibacy, it is a laughing matter — and to fail to see the comedy of grace which it entails is to miss its deeper religious truth. Every attempt to make a reasonable claim for priestly celibacy not only robs it of the foolishness that makes it livable as a faith commitment, but also misses the divine sense of humor encoded in it.

A good sense of humor is needed to live and "see through" the obligation of priestly celibacy: not just any kind of humor, but that comic perception of life which only a strong faith can give. When seen through the eyes of faith, there is something inherently laughable about the connection the Church makes between priest-hood and celibacy. On the one hand, we priests are asked to love the people we serve and to whom we minister with a deep, all-consuming, compassionate love. On the other hand, we are asked to do this without the benefit or assistance of that part of our anatomy so well suited for expressing love, namely, our genitalia. Our predicament is not unlike that of Abraham, for both stem from the same faith and the same obedience. Without the laughter of faith, priestly celibacy either becomes an intolerable burden or degenerates into cynicism and callous boredom. Without the comic vision of faith, any reason advanced for defending priestly celibacy will invariably appear contrived, stilted, and unconvincing.

In short, what distinguishes Christian laughter from ordinary profane laughter is not what we laugh at, but the faith vision that prompts us to laugh. It is precisely because Chaucer was a good Christian and a man of faith that he could poke fun at the Monk and the Prioress, the lecherous Friar and the Pardner with his sack full of indulgences "hot from Rome." Without the vision of faith, it is unlikely that Chaucer would have regarded these characters as a laughing matter; most probably he would have seen them as a real threat to the Church to be met by invective witch-hunts. The perceived incongruity that results in Christian laughter is always rooted in the gift of faith.

Endnotes

1. G.K. Chesterton, *St. Francis of Assisi* (New York: George H. Doran, 1924), p. 176.
2. Eugene O'Neill, *Nine Plays* (New York: Garden City Publishing, 1940), p. 418.
3. W. H. Auden, *Collected Longer Poems* (New York: Random House, 1969), p. 175.
4. See Conrad Hyers, "The Dialectic of the Sacred and the Comic," *Cross Currents* 19 (Winter 1969): 74.
5. Rudolph Otto, *The Idea of the Holy*, trans. John W. Harvey (London: Oxford University Press, 1923), pp. 8-41.

Laughter in our daily faith   8

> *We have paid and are paying a price for forgetting the role of laughter in Christian living. The person who laughs remains free.*
>
> — Gerald O'Collins

THE TASK OF THIS CHAPTER is to uncover some practical applications of the theology of laughter and what might result if this theology were effectively translated into our everyday life of faith. It is not enough to understand the foundations and general principles of our theology; theory is important, but not everything. Our theology, if genuine, must be able to transform the thinking believer who thereby becomes leaven in the world. Having been changed interiorly by accepting God's mirth, the believer will radiate it and become a principle of hope and conversion for others. In order to insure this result, we cannot remain abstract, alienated from life, or detached from Christian existence. Hence I will indicate some specific areas where a theology of laughter can influence our daily faith and help us to possess it in a more vibrant way.

A good way to begin is to ask the question, "What would change in my life or my ministry if I took seriously this theology of laughter, if I surrendered to the symbol of a laughing God?"

A positive vision

The first and most obvious way the laughter of faith will transform our lives and ministry is to help us choose and sustain a positive outlook. How we handle demanding situations in life or in ministry is largely determined by our appraisal of their potential stress. Studies in stress management indicate that a situation only becomes harmfully stressful to us when we perceive it in a negative way. In a very real sense, stress begins in the eye of the beholder. We cannot change significantly the society, church, and ministerial environment in which we live, but we can alter our perception of them, as well as our relationship to them.

Here holy mirth can be most beneficial. It frees us from negative appraisal of events that leads to worry, tension, and stress, and reminds us that God, not we, is ultimately "in charge of the store." I am again reminded of the holy wit and wisdom of Pope John XXIII. On the night before he announced the convocation of Vatican Council II, he experienced some difficulty in falling asleep because of nervous tension — with good reason, since many of his closest advisers in the Curia were opposed to the idea. Because of his deeply Christian sense of humor, he suddenly realized God's ultimate providential influence in the whole matter and was able to talk himself to sleep thus: "Giovanni, why don't you sleep? Is it the Pope or the Holy Spirit who governs the Church? It is the Holy Spirit, no? Well, then, go to sleep, Giovanni."

A good laugh releases physical and mental tension. Some people, like Dr. Hendrie Weisinger, contend that if we do not laugh at least fifteen times a day we are not laughing enough. However, the essential point is not how frequently we laugh, but the overall positive vision that comes with a discovery of God's humor, a vision most helpful in alleviating the real stress in our lives and ministry. While a certain amount of stress is necessary in motivating us to be creative in ministry, too much stress yoked to a negative outlook threatens our effectiveness. It can dampen our enthusiasm for ministering to others and ruin our health. Stress becomes unmanageable when our usual frame of mind is characterized by pessimism, lack of faith, disdain for modern society, or nostalgia for the "good old days" in the Church.

Pope John's holy mirth made him see things more positively. When he opened the Second Vatican Council on October 11, 1962, he stated to the 2,600 Council members in unusually forceful language: "In the daily exercise of our pastoral office our ears are shocked, much to our regret, by the voices of persons who, though burning with religious zeal, . . . can see nothing but calamities and ruin. They say that our era, in comparison with past eras, is getting worse . . . . We feel we must declare our total disagreement with these prophets of doom who always foretell catastrophes as though the world were close to its end."[1] Nothing was more foreign to Pope John's positive view of the world, of the Church, and of people generally. His was a different vision, a vision enhanced by God's contagious mirth.

An "open" ministerial style

An extension of this idea of a positive outlook is the need for an "open" ministerial style. In America one of the most highly rated expectations of pastoral ministers is an open, affirming style. This view emerges in a recent report, based on an in-depth survey conducted among laity and clergy of forty-seven denominations in the United States and Canada. The report, called *Ministry in America*, is the fruit of a six-year project undertaken by The Association of Theological Schools in the United States and Canada. The findings of this report reveal that of all the expectations that people have about their priests or ministers, the one that consistently received the highest rating of importance was "an open, affirming style."

What exactly does this statement mean? As used in this report, an open, affirming style includes a core cluster of defining characteristics and criteria, each of which was highly valued and rated in the top category of importance for ministry. Among these characteristics were the following:

- *Positive approach.* Handling stressful situations by remaining calm under pressure while continuing to affirm persons.
- *Flexibility of spirit.* Adaptability, balance, free sharing of views, and welcoming of new possibilities.
- *Acknowledgment of limitations.* Acknowledging limitations and mistakes, and recognizing the need for continued growth and learning.
- *Valuing diversity.* Strong enough acceptance and valuation of diversity in people and ideas to face the risks involved in changes.

This aggregate of personal qualities for ministry can easily leave the priest or minister discouraged. "How can I possibly live up to these expectations? Should I even try?" Yet to the extent that these ministerial qualities suggest wisdom and love, caring and competence, affirmation and grace, they must be respected as meaningful goals in ministry. They are also directly called forth and sustained by the laughter of faith.

We have already seen the importance of holy mirth in maintaining a positive outlook and reducing the danger of stress and burnout. The connection between holy mirth and flexibility of spirit is also quite obvious, especially as it pertains to adaptability and the perception of new possibilities (see chapter 6). One of the gifts of holy mirth is the grace of flexibility. A believer who is in touch with the blessed reversals of God's humor will not be unyielding, intractable, or unwilling to compromise. Nor will such a person fall into the "controller" syndrome, that tendency of trying to force something to happen without sharing some of the decision-making in ministry and pastoral responsibility.

Those who are unable to laugh with God will find it very difficult to let go of their priestly or ministerial prerogatives. They

will want to be in charge, not trusting others to handle matters.
They will find it difficult to give wholehearted support to lay
leaders in the Church, or to face the risks involved in significant
changes. An open, affirming style in ministry is only possible if we
are able to appreciate the comic predicament in which our faith has
placed us. This is especially true when it comes to acknowledging
our personal limitations and mistakes in ministry.

If the laughter of faith provides any grace or blessings for
ministry, it is surely the ability to laugh at our own human frailty
as followers of Christ. When a priest has celebrated the Eucharist,
administered the sacraments, or preached the word of God, he then
needs a good deal of holy mirth to take his place among his lay
listeners. For example, after preaching a homily on the parable of
the sower, the priest should ask himself if he is not the soil on
which the seed was wasted because it fell by the wayside, or the soil
hardened by routine, or the soil that stifled the good seed under the
thorns of worldly cares and preoccupations. In short, holy mirth
excludes no one, not even the close follower or minister of Christ.
It will always raise the question that was on the lips of the first
apostles: "Surely it is not I, Lord?" (Matt. 26:22).

An antidote to boredom

Holy mirth can change our lives and ministry in yet another
way: it relieves us of spiritual boredom. Like stress, spiritual
boredom is a real danger in ministry. Human nature being what it
is, we tire of the same acts through frequent repetition, even when
they are sacred, like celebrating the Eucharist or the Liturgy of the
Hours, or even when the action is blessed, like feeding the hungry,
welcoming the stranger, comforting the sick, or visiting prisoners
(see Matt. 25:31-46). Any priest who has been assigned the early
morning mass in a parish on a regular basis will know what I mean.
So will the religious education teacher who meets the same class
week after week. I think even the Pope must get bored with his job

at times, at least with some aspects of it—perhaps the pressing crowds, the burden of public exposure, the length of papal ceremonies, or the panoply of medieval pageantry.

The point I wish to stress is that our faith and the ministry that flows from it do not of themselves immunize us against boredom. Even the apostles, we are told, fell asleep at a crucial turning point in Jesus' ministry. The spiritual boredom I am describing here is the dreary sadness of a heart that is unable to accept the greatness of the present moment, the dull inertia that makes us lose sight of the nobility of routine ministry. When we become euphoric because it is Friday afternoon and depressed because it is Sunday night, our behavior reveals significant feelings about our work. How can we prevent our ministry from becoming stereotyped, mechanical, and routine?

Part of the answer lies in our quest for holy mirth. In chapter 6 I talked about "the sanctification of trivia." We saw how some of God's choicest blessings and humor come in the ordinary, uneventful things that make up our daily lives. Holy mirth keeps us alert to the thrilling moments of "dull" routine. As a rule we are not bored with papal visits. The Pope does not come to our country that often. When he does come, the occasion is always event-filled. We get caught up in a swirl of anticipation, local church routines are broken, and our faith is again quickened. Such inspiring graces, however, are brief and rare. In the long interims our souls are often dull, bare, and vapid. But they need not be if we are on the same wavelength as God's sense of humor. With God, even the most routine visit can turn into a thrilling papal visit.

Time and again in Jesus' own ministry, many things seem to occur by chance in the daily routine of his rounds. For instance, we are told that the healing of the blind man at Siloam took place "as Jesus was passing by" (John 9:1). We do not get the impression that Jesus went out looking for people to heal. He healed when the opportunity presented itself. How many important things happen in our own pastoral ministry not because of a prearranged plan, but because God has a greater sense of humor than we do?

The deep truth and beauty of God's humor is that routine breeds opportunity, not boredom, and calls forth a response where our soul might otherwise remain dormant. God delights in the unexpected and the unlikely, and because of this, God is especially delight-full to those who appreciate the divine sense of humor. For God, there is no such thing as a routine visit, a regular schedule, an ordinary exchange, or a repeatable moment. The reason, as we have seen, is because ours is a God of the improbable, full of surprises, highly unconventional, and blissfully spontaneous. Is it any wonder, therefore, that Christians of every generation have been warned to be vigilant? I have often fancied that what the early Christians expected in the imminent Parousia has something to do with God's immanent humor. In the same way that we do not know when the Second Coming will take place, we are in the dark as to when God will play his next practical joke on us. Whoever has experienced God's humor will surely want to heed the gospel advice, "Be constantly on the watch! Stay awake! You do not know when the appointed time will come" (Mark 13:33).

An antidote to gullibility

Holy mirth also makes us less gullible. Any Christian who has heard God laugh at least once will be much more prone to think and feel in what might be called a critical mood, or in a critical key, to borrow a musical symbol. Such a Christian will no longer take things at face value, or believe something because it is accepted or announced by the majority (whether it be the vocal or silent majority). If holy mirth teaches us anything, it is to be wary about the unanimous agreement of others, especially the popular consensus of the marketplace. In the light of God's humor, the exact contrary of what is generally believed is often the truth. Hence all surface judgments, clichés, slogans, and appeals to "common sense" become ludicrous in the eyes of the believer. Nothing can be taken for granted or at face value.

We need not look far to see a prevalent tendency toward gullibility in our society, and it would be foolish to think that any of us is immune to it. We see in advertising how people are led to purchase a product because a television or newspaper ad pronounces it better than any other. Modern day advertisers even use humor in their ads to appear more sincere and so more credible. Their basic claim, "What you see is what you get," is another untrustworthy slogan since what we see is rarely, if ever, what we do get.

The same softmindedness appears in the tendency of many people to accept the printed word of the press as final truth. Who would deny that we believe much, if not most, of what we read (including, I might add, these very pages)? Yet holy mirth would remind us that even our best channels of information — the press, the platform, the pulpit — can never deliver the final word about anything. The reason should be obvious: beneath and behind every human word, printed or spoken, there is always the ironic presence of God's humor that invites us to take everything "with a grain of salt" — except Him.

Those who have never seen through God's humor are convinced that the truth is obvious, that everyone should agree, and that things really are the way they appear to be. The believer who knows God's humor thinks differently, thinks in a critical mood. This critical mood is not cynicism, but it offers an insight into reality, in contrast to the half-truths and fictions that are often substituted for reality. A person who never doubts may have a serenity and self-assurance we admire; sometimes we see this in older people, perhaps our parents or grandparents. But someone who never doubts may also become a very dogmatic person. There is no room for another viewpoint, for dialogue, for listening to and learning from others. Yet the Christian posture encouraged by God's laughter does not propagate, but contradicts conventional wisdom, stereotypes, prejudices, and ideological certitudes. Like Penelope, it undoes each night the tapestry that public opinion wove the day before. It also shatters the inadequate conceptions of

God that linger unconsciously in our minds and prevent us from catching a glimpse of the true God.

Endnote

1. Quoted in *Wit and Wisdom of Good Pope John*, collected by Henri Fesquet (New York: P.J. Kenedy and Sons, 1964), pp. 135-136.

The courage to laugh   9

We must be bold and courageous, for
God helps the strong.

— St. Therese

I WOULD LIKE TO BEGIN this final chapter with an example taken from my years as a missionary in Southern Africa.

Looking at some pictures taken during the 1976 Soweto riots just outside of Johannesburg, especially those of the massive street demonstrations that took place in that township, one notices immediately the number of defiant students who took part in the demonstration as well as the burst of laughter on their lips. It was the laughing students who struck most terror into the hearts of their oppressors. Although it may have been the misery and the injustice around them that made them laugh, the students' laughter had an intensely liberating effect on the country. For the children of Soweto, laughing was a profound affirmation of life, a heroic gesture of defiance in the face of South Africa's crushing tragedies. Through their laughter, one could detect an unquenchable nobility of spirit that refused to let an unjust system of government have the last word. In this sense, a preliminary victory over cynicism and despair was already won. Moreover, this laughter of youth and innocence was the prophetic kind of laughter which tyrants fear so much precisely because it comes, as the truth often does, from the mouths of babes. Such laughter exposes, as nothing else can, the lies, illusions, and sacrosanct principles of an unjust system. So the children of Soweto laughed — and their laughter was heard around the world. This illustration introduces us to the prophetic function of Christian laughter. Like the children of Soweto, Christians today must learn to laugh before the gods of our society — the gods of conformism, of apathy, of material success, of exploitive power, of racism, and of war. These idols are worshipped by many people in our society, and Christians must find the courage to laugh in these deceiving faces. Unless we learn to laugh with God, who invariably has the last laugh on every issue that confronts us, our Christian faith can never truly liberate our society.

Prophets and reformers of every generation (Martin Luther is a notable example) have always armed themselves with the shield of humor and the weapon of laughter. Many abuses which resist the combined assaults of reason, argument, and denunciation yield to the genial onslaught of humor and fly before its shouts of laughter. Prophetic laughter is sometimes the only way to unmask the false prudence and cunning of those who shirk the test of Jesus' gospel and who fear to "proclaim the truth openly" (2 Cor. 4:2). Laughter cuts deeply into those safe games people play, useless for real encounters with God and genuine openness to one's neighbor. When a prophet laughs, it is to keep people and nations from falling into or remaining in ruts of injustice. Even in the face of insuperable odds, the prophet laughs for one purpose: to affirm life and the possibility of hope. As Harvey Cox puts it: "Only by learning to laugh at the hopelessness around us can we touch the hem of hope."[1]

When people laugh at their oppressors, as they often do in times of persecution or under repressive regimes, they are avoiding total and utter subjugation. Surely, the ultimate oppression comes when we begin to think like our oppressors, when we take on their flawed ideology and view the world and ourselves as they do. In his book called *Laughing Matter*, George Mikes makes the following astute observation:

> If you take your oppressors and persecutors seri-
> ously—you will, sooner or later, take over their
> valuation of yourself, you will feel guilty and will see
> yourself through their eyes. Take the despots
> seriously and you will be broken by them and you
> will, eventually, perish. But if you are able to laugh
> at them—see their stupidity, their vanity and
> meanness—if you realize the fatuity of their claims to
> superiority—then oppression will steel you, make
> you stronger, more united as a group, and victory—
> or at least liberation—becomes possible.[2]

As we can see, this kind of aggressive humor, this laughing at one's oppressor, is not absent in the history of Christian spirituality. In fact, there is at least one area in our tradition where such aggressive humor is not only present, but even prescribed by many of the saints we venerate, namely, laughing at the devil. In Christian tradition, laughter and mockery are effective means to overcome evil temptations. We see this behavior in the holy antics of the desert ascetics of the fourth century. They would laugh and stick their tongue out at the devil, calling him such comically defiant epithets as "toothless asp," "swashbuckler," "the harmless one," and so on. As one of them wryly put it, "We fear the flies here even more than the demons."

In order to appreciate better this comic tradition, we should remember that the desert was not regarded as a refuge or a safe haven from the world, much less a place of serenity. Nor did these ascetics consider their solitary sojourn in the wilderness as a privileged place of encounter with God, a quiet retreat, where God was expected to speak more assuredly and more directly to an individual. Quite the contrary! The desert was for them a place to do battle, a forbidding and secluded area where demons roamed freely—not unlike the time when Jesus went into the wilderness and was tempted by Satan. Here, in the fearsome wilderness, the desert ascetics could measure themselves and their strength against the Evil One. And they did so, not only with prayer and fasting, but also with a remarkable sense of humor and aggressive laughter. Laughing at the devil thus came to be regarded as an effective remedy against evil temptations and not a few spiritual writers, like St. Bernard, St. Catherine of Sienna, and St. Teresa, have recommended it. As Martin Luther so often insisted, "The best way to drive out the devil, if he will not yield to texts of Scripture, is to jeer and flout him, for he cannot bear scorn." This sentiment was shared by Thomas More who was tempted to commit suicide in his prison tower but instead found the courage to laugh.

Belief in the existence of demons and their action in the world has declined in our day and age, and the evils once attributed to demons are now understood in different ways. Nevertheless, we should not lose sight of the fact that demons did represent in a mythological way some truths about evil which even today cannot be ignored. Among these truths are the depth and mystery of evil in the world; the superhuman dimensions of evil; its sometimes apparently systemic character; the fact that evil is so pervasive it is often hard to recognize; and the knowledge that courage is necessary to confront the horrifying wickedness we see at work in humanity. We live in a world in which the power of evil is formidable. Those who know the world well, realize the terrifying ravages of moral disorders. They know that the "mystery of iniquity" (2 Thess. 2:7) is no less perplexing today than it was in the days of Paul. Besides moral evil there is physical evil, and the suffering it entails is closely bound up with sin. According to the Bible, it was sin that brought suffering into the world, and suffering continues to be in many ways the wages of sin.

Although our ideas about the devil may be quite different today, the reality and mystery of evil are still powerfully present in our world; and it does not matter by what terms we designate them. The question is not whether demons really exist, and, if so, what their nature might be, nor is the problem the lack of realism, of underestimating the contagious power of evil in the world. For a Christian, the only question is "What stand must I take in the face of evil? What is my basic response?" To remain neutral or indifferent is clearly an unacceptable option. As Dante vividly put it: "The hottest places in Hell are reserved for those who, in a time of great moral crisis, maintain their neutrality." Revelation is no less graphic: "Because you are lukewarm, and neither hot nor cold, I will spit you out of my mouth" (3:16).

Every Christian, then, must oppose and resist evil under whatever guise it presents itself. The theology of laughter I propose here is one option (although not the only one). It should be clear from the outset, however, that whatever strategy or form of resistance we choose, our basic inner disposition will be one of humility and holy fear. Nothing alarms us more than a man or woman ostensibly devoid of fear. The person who recklessly and indiscriminately courts danger is not brave or courageous, nor is he or she necessarily a true prophet. In fact, one of the signs by which we recognize a false prophet is the presence of a blind, exuberant, daredevil spirit, one that denies the awesome power of evil or its capacity to enslave or pervert even the best and the strongest amongst us. In dealing with the forces of evil, therefore, the Christian is not a dreamer but a realist, one who is ever mindful of the fearfulness of evil as well as its seductiveness.

Traditionally, the devil was represented in early Christian art under two principle forms, Horror and Beauty. On the one hand, the devil (or evil) was depicted as an ugly, monstrous being who frightens and attacks people, a repugnant, repulsive spirit (not unlike the one portrayed in the film *The Exorcist*). The devil was also depicted as a beguiling, tempting creature, representing all the enticements of the world, a person of astounding beauty, a handsome, charming young man or woman, or an angel of light. The early Christians recognized that evil can be so attractive and seductive that people do in fact consent to its temptation. The appropriate symbol for evil, some felt, had to be personal and appealing; it had to appear as something good.

Another important point to remember is that whenever evil presents itself to us, whether as something attractive or fearsome, a prudent decision is needed as to whether it is better to flee or fight. Both options are legitimate and both can be prophetic. The real prophet is not only one who stands and directly confronts evil like a David who takes on a Goliath, but also one who knows when to flee as Jesus did. He slipped away from the crowd that would stone him, and let Judas' conspiracy to betray him run its course without interference or resistance. Too often, we restrict the prophetic voices of our day to those who participate in direct confrontation by marching, picketing, boycotting, and attending protest rallies. We forget the numerous Christians who turn their back on evil, have nothing to do with it, and thus choose to break solidarity with evil through flight rather than fight. These people can be called the quiet prophets. They do not make the headlines nor do they capture prime time on national television news. But they are all around us, if we but open our eyes and see that the Kingdom of God is perhaps much more at hand than we realize.

Prophetic laughter represents a relatively unexplored strategy or form of resistance to evil, and it is this neglected dimension of Christian laughter I wish to stress here. One reason a person needs courage to laugh in the face of evil or wrong doing is because of its subversive nature. It exposes human beings and societies for what they are in contrast to what they profess to be. As Hyers puts it, "The comic spirit is iconoclastic, and in that sense has a genuinely prophetic dimension . . . it topples our various idols, punctures high-flying balloons, and kicks pompous asses."[3] Prophetic laughter is an effective nonviolent way to unveil some of the false values of our society. It is not enough to laugh at the innocent foibles of life; we must also laugh at the real evil that confronts our day and age. This action goes against our sensitivities: serious evil, we feel, should be seriously dealt with — not laughed at. But such behavior gives Christian laughter its prophetic quality. The prophetic function does not exist in a vacuum. In general it is founded on an implicit or explicit criticism of a personal situation or of unjust circumstances in a society. It arises as a protest, and its critical aspect is a sudden awareness of the intolerable, a debunking of the excuses that preserve it, and a refusal to let oneself be manipulated. As with every other form of resistance, prophetic laughter marks a deliberate break with evil; it refuses to yield to the subjugating forces of evil and breaks solidarity with them. Like the children of Soweto, whose laughter was heard around the world, Christians must become conscientious objectors in their innermost beings; when confronted with evil, their Christian conscience must concentrate on a radical refusal. This inner refusal, which can only take place in the hidden depths of one's heart and conscience, then issues forth in that sudden unique response — a burst of prophetic laughter. At that moment, often for the first time, a Christian comes to understand the deeper meaning and comfort of Jesus' words: "In the world you will find suffering, but have courage: I have conquered the world" (John 16: 33).

Endnotes

1. Harvey Cox, *The Feast of Fools* (Cambridge, Mass.: Harvard University Press, 1969), pp. 156-157.
2. George Mikes, *Laughing Matter* (New York: Library Press, 1970), p. 111.
3. Conrad Hyers, "The Comic Vision in a Tragic World," *The Christian Century* (April 20, 1983): 366.

Bibliography

Adams, Doug. *Humor in the American Pulpit*. North Aurora, Ill.: The Sharing Company, 1975.

Berger, Peter. *The Precarious Vision*. Garden City, N.Y.: Doubleday, 1961.

—— *A Rumor of Angels*. Garden City, N.Y.: Doubleday, 1970.

Bessiere, Gerard. "Humor—A Theological Attitude?" *Concilium*, New Series, 5 (1974): 81-95.

Buechner, Frederick. *Telling the Truth*. New York: Harper and Row, 1977, especially "The Gospel as Comedy," pp. 49-72.

Cox, Harvey. *The Feast of Fools*. Cambridge, Mass.: Harvard University Press, 1969, especially "Christianity as Comedy," pp. 149-157.

Crossan, John D. *The Dark Interval*. Niles, Ill.: Argus Communications, 1975, especially "Parable and Humor," pp. 93- 101.

——. *Raid on the Articulate: Comic Eschatology in Jesus and Borges*. New York: Harper and Row, 1976.

Flugel, J.C. "Humor and Laughter." *Handbook of Social Psychology*. Ed. Gardner Lindzey. Volume 2. Reading, Mass.: Addison-Wesley Publishing Company, 1954.

Greeley, Andrew. "Humor and Ecclesiastical Ministry." *Concilium*, New Series, 5 (1974):134-140.

Haring, Bernard. *Free and Faithful in Christ*. Volume 2. New York: Seabury Press, 1979, especially "Sense of Humor," pp. 145-148.

Hyers, Conrad. *The Comic Vision and the Christian Faith*. Princeton, N.J.: Pilgrim Press, 1982.

Kronenberger, Louis. *Company Manners: A Cultural Inquiry Into Modern American Life*. New York: Bobbs-Merrill, 1962, especially "The American Sense of Humor," pp. 145-148.

Lynch, William. *Christ and Apollo*. New York: Sheed and Ward, 1960, especially "Comedy," pp. 99-117.

Mikes, George. *Laughing Matter*. New York: Library Press, 1971.

Niebuhr, Reinhold. *Discerning the Signs of the Times.* New York: Charles Scribner's Sons, 1946, especially "Humor and Faith," pp. 11-131.

Polhemus, Robert. *Comic Faith: The Great Tradition From Austen to Joyce.* Chicago: University of Chicago Press, 1980.

Rahner, Karl. *Belief Today.* New York: Sheed and Ward, 1967, especially "On Laughter," pp. 29-31.

Trueblood, Elton. *The Humor of Christ.* New York: Harper and Row, 1964.

Affirmation Books is am important part of the ministry of the House of Affirmation, International Therapeutic Center for Clergy and Religious, founded by Sr. Anna Polcino, M.D., F.A.P.A., and Fr. Thomas A. Kane, Ph.D., D.P.S. Income from the sale of Affirmation books and tapes is used to provide care for priests and religious suffering from emotional unrest.

The House of Affirmation provides a threefold program of service, education, and research. Among its services are five residential therapeutic communities and three counseling centers in the United States and one residential center in England. All centers provide nonresidential counseling.

The Affirmation Center for Education offers a variety of sabbatical and continuing education programs in ongoing Christian formation. It sponsors a leadership conference each year during the first week of February and a month-long Institute of Applied Psychotheology during July. More than forty clinical staff members conduct workshops and symposiums throughout the year.

For further information, write or call the administrative offices in Natick, Massachusetts:

> The House of Affirmation
> 109 Woodland Street
> Natick, Massachusetts 01760
> 617/651-3893